NOVICE in the NORTH

William M. Robinson

payak - neesyou - nisto (1, 2, 3)
ogamassis (little boss)
moona neena (not me)
ogamau (boss)
kewatin (north wind)

NOVICE in the NORTH

William M. Robinson

hancock

house

ISBN 0-88839-977-4

Typeset by Elizabeth Grant in Souvenir
    on AM Varityper Comp/Edit
Production by Dorothy Forbes,
    production assistant Jane Gueho
Illustrations by Dorothy Forbes
Cover photo by Dr. Andrew Farquhar,
    courtesy of NFB Phototheque
Printed in Canada by Friesen Printers

Published simultaneously in Canada and the United States by

HANCOCK HOUSE PUBLISHERS LTD.
19313 Zero Ave., Surrey, B.C. V3S 5J9
HANCOCK HOUSE PUBLISHERS INC.
1431 Harrison Avenue, Blaine, WA 98230

Contents

To Ruby

Acknowledgements

My thanks to *The Beaver, The Western Producer* and *north/nord* for their permission to again use some of this material.

I Have a Job

"This looks like an excellent position and your qualifications will make you an excellent candidate for it." The school principal's words as he handed me the application form indicated he felt my chances of obtaining employment were far greater than my personal survey of the job market led me to believe.

The fact that he took the trouble to drive the four miles from the town of Souris, Manitoba, to my parent's farm reinforced the enthusiasm he showed in his voice. I quickly looked at the application form. "This will be in the mail by this afternoon," I assured him.

No sooner had he left than I began to complete the form. It was for a job with the Fur Trade Department of the Hudson's Bay Company. The job offered a way of life that few men ever experienced. I completed the form far more enthusiastically than I had ever previously filled out one before. If the employment picture had been so favorable that I could have selected any position, I am certain I would still have applied for this job.

At that period in history, working for wages was a condition only the fortunate few enjoyed. In 1938, working for relief chits was the order of the day. Applications submitted to industrial firms were seldom, if ever, answered. Twice I stood naked in a recruiting centre and failed to progress any further than the eye chart during my enlistment endeavors. It appeared the chances of finding steady work were approximately the same as the chances of winning a lottery when you did not have a ticket.

The Hudson's Bay Company, however, was actually looking for help. The school principal was correct in his assessment. Within two weeks I received a reply which set a date when I should be present in Winnipeg for an interview. If the company interviewers so decided, I would remain in the city and spend four months attending a training school. After this four-month period of preliminary training, the graduating apprentices would be posted to an arctic or a subarctic post.

However, regardless of the outcome of the interview, I would be reimbursed for the expenses I incurred in making the trip. I had a sure winner in the job-seeking lottery. Even if I did not get the big prize, the expense-paid trip from Souris to Manitoba's capital would be an excellent consolation prize.

I had two days to make preparations. Everyone I told of my good fortune expressed the same envious thought: "They will pay good money. They will have to in order to get anyone to go there."

I did not argue or divulge the quoted rate. By some standards it could have been considered far from good. However, to a Depression-era farm boy who had spent a good portion of his life scheming how he could manage to leave the farm, the chance to live in the far north presented the opportunity of a lifetime. The satisfaction of obtaining employment other than farm laboring eliminated all concern about the rate of pay. To me, the quoted rate of twenty dollars per month plus board constituted a good wage. The previous winter, by taking advantage of the government's make-work program, I worked at a neighboring farm which paid five dollars per month and board. Four hundred per cent raises in spending power were not common during the Depression, when some unions agreed to cutbacks.

The few dollars I managed to earn during the summer were already spent on winter clothes. My worldly wealth consisted of two dollars and twenty cents. I didn't have the where-with-all to ride in style. The freight train schedule with its disembarking problems placed riding one out of the question. I began to canvass the truckers and salesmen that I knew who might be making a trip to the city. It seemed that September 1938 was my lucky month. The second person I asked said he would be glad to have my company. He planned to leave for Winnipeg the following morning at five o'clock with a truckload of pigs.

The well-graded gravel road to Winnipeg enabled us to make excellent time. We covered the 180 miles in just over seven hours. My benefactor had a favorite hotel where we both booked rooms. Fortunately, I was carrying luggage so payment could be made when I checked out rather than in advance. The trucker immediately went about his business and I took advantage of the running water to freshen up before I presented myself for that all-important interview.

During the interview, three interviewers made separate assessments of me. All three were talkative but I was taciturn. However, I made the right impression. Even though I might criticize the loquaciousness of one of the interviewers, I would never criticize his judgement.

The next morning, at seven o'clock, we met at our preselected rendezvous where I told my truck driver friend, "I'm staying here. I've got a job."

The training school paid ten dollars a week to defray expenses. Room and board at the boarding house which the training school recommended cost twenty-five dollars a month. Therefore, I had fifteen dollars per month left over for incidentals. I could already consider the Depression a condition I suffered through during my younger years.

We were not told how many applications the Hudson's Bay Company received. We did learn that over 600 prospects were interviewed at company centres across Canada. Of that number, fourteen people were selected to start the training school; eleven of us graduated.

We were taught the basics of accounting, fur grading, merchandising, carpentry, meteorology and sufficient radio theory to qualify us for a private commercial licence. After the third week, a night school course was added to the curriculum; every Monday and every Wednesday evening we attended a special cooking class at Daniel McIntyre Collegiate.

Finally, graduation day arrived. Instead of diplomas we received outpost assignments. The farewell address was short and sweet. Simply stated it said: "Go home 'til we call you."

I was assigned to York Factory. Travel arrangements allowed me to spend three weeks at home before I was called to start work.

The Journey North

The journey from Winnipeg to York Factory was taken in three stages of decreasing luxury. The first stage was a trip in a first-class train coach from Winnipeg to The Pas. The second stage saw people, express, mail and freight transported from The Pas to Gillam in some poor, forgotten relative of a train. The third stage marked the end of modern travel and the beginning of northern romance as dog teams provided the only winter link between Gillam and York Factory.

I was given my tickets, ten dollars expense money, and the usual bon voyage messages from the training school staff. Although I made every effort to appear nonchalant, traveling first class on a train was in itself a new adventure for me. Most of my previous traveling had been via railroad with all the luxuries an empty boxcar could provide. To make the overnight trip to The Pas I had a berth, access to the parlor car, and money in my pocket.

I had not added tobacco to my list of cravings, but even so I spent most of my time in the smokers' lounge. The furnishings in the lounge were more luxurious than most of the furnishings in the houses I had visited. A deep pile rug covered the floor, separate easy chairs were placed at strategic positions throughout the car and a well-stocked magazine rack offered a selection of the latest periodicals. I silently assessed the value of the clothing worn by the other men occupying the car. Compared to my eleven dollar and ninety-five cent mail-order suit and my two dollar bargain-basement shoes, these men were expensively dressed. I promised myself that the next time I rode the train I too would wear thirty dollar made-to-measure suits and seven dollar and fifty cent shoes.

When the porter came to make up my lower bunk, sleep was the farthest thing from my mind. I felt certain I would experience a long and restless night as I wormed my way in between the sheets. However, the rhythmic clatter of the wheels against the rails combined with the motion of the train lulled me into dreamland almost immediately.

Long before I felt ready to begin experiencing the adventures of another day, the noise of bustling activity just outside my berth window made me aware that we had arrived at an important station. I peeked out the window from the edge of the blind and saw the words "The Pas" in big letters on the end of a building.

I threw back the covers and began to dress. What if I had overslept and missed the train to Gillam? I hurriedly picked up my baggage and alighted. Even the porter had apparently left the coach.

The activity on the station platform seemed to belie the existence of the Depression. Loaded express and baggage carts blocked passage along the entire length of the platform. I eased my way through the express and the baggage handling equipment and made my way along a road to the station entrance. I noticed this northern town boasted at least two hotels. A sign on a four-seated bus offered transportation to one of these hotels, while a sign on a passenger car offered transportation to another.

I entered the station and inquired when the train left for Gillam. I learned I had a twenty-four-hour wait. I also learned if I wished to continue on to Churchill I would have a three-week wait. During the winter the train visited Manitoba's seaport only on the last week of every month.

Now I realized why I was given such a large expense fund. I would have to patronize one of the local hotels. By the time I left the station the passenger bus had already disappeared. The rear of the departing bus showed me the general direction to walk. With a suitcase in each hand I started walking — my destination proved to be only four blocks distant.

The outer appearance of the hotel gave every assurance that its rates would be within my traveling budget. After I registered, the clerk led me to my room. He opened the door, switched on the light and explained where I would find the bathroom. By the time I realized he'd neglected to provide me with a key, he was long gone. I took a walk to the bathroom and noted that none of the other rooms had locks. Half an hour in the hotel room proved sufficient to make me feel restless. I decided to break the monotony and explore the town.

The temperature was slightly warmer than it was in Winnipeg the day before. However, everyone I met on the street from toddler to grandparent, wore clothes designed to provide protection from a severe climate. I suddenly realized that parkas, like topcoats, came in styles which could be worn for work, for dress or for any function in between. Genuine Indian moccasins with duffle boots for linings seemed to be the accepted footwear. While I noticed the parkas and the moccasins, the mitts really caught my attention. I had dreamed of owning a pair of big, leather gauntlet mitts ever since my boyhood days. Here in The Pas it seemed everybody except me wore them. Some were plain, some had elaborate beadwork designs and some had fringes, but I envied the wearer in every case. I began to think of reasons that would justify spending the six dollars and fifty cents which remained from my expense fund after I paid for my room. Finally, I let security override vanity; mitts would be the first purchase I would make when I received my first pay.

At seven o'clock the next morning I arrived at the station eager to begin the second stage of my journey. Several trains were positioned on the maze of tracks. Some trains gave the impression they had just arrived. Others, with their engines hissing steam, gave the impression they were preparing to depart. However, unlike the transportation which the hotels provided, none of the trains displayed signs informing people of their destination. I enquired which was the northbound train on the Hudson Bay railway. A bystander took me to task for my use of that name. The Muskeg Express or the Blueberry Special were acceptable titles, but never the Hudson Bay railway.

I found my way to the train which stood on the track furthest from the station. I entered a coach with "first class" clearly written in big, gold letters along its side. The first-class coach that provided my transportation from The Pas greatly differed from the one that brought me there. I reached up, pulled a handle and expected to open a luggage compartment. Instead, I found I had opened the upper berth. Since it looked more suitable for carrying luggage than for slumbering passengers, I placed my bags on its wooden floor. I eased myself into the wicker-covered seat and immediately thought of the grain sack filled with hay which I used back on the farm to reduce the shock from cold implement seats. A sudden, severe jolt informed all on board that the engine was connected to the Muskeg Express.

The passenger list consisted of five men other than myself. As I looked at the clothing they wore I immediately felt slightly overdressed and improperly dressed to the extreme. All five of my companions wore heavy, black woolen sweaters and black denim trousers. They all wore heavy shirts open at the neck, but the shirts showed the wearers had some individuality as they all varied in color.

No sooner had the train started than one of my fellow passengers seated himself beside me. "You must be Bill Robinson on your way to York," he said. Then he decided to complete the introduction and continued: "My name's John."

I looked at him in amazement. He answered my inquiring gaze: "News travels fast in this country. I heard the agent tell Waboden that you were on the train."

The sound of voices gained the attention of the other people in the coach. As soon as they noticed I was wearing a suit and tie they moved into the adjacent seats. Although I cannot deny their welcome to the north, they were also able, willing and exceptionally eager to indulge in the age old game of spoofing the tenderfoot.

One chap first looked at my luggage and then looked at me with an expression of utter disbelief. "You dunna have a sleeping robe laddie." He did not need to tell me his name because with that accent it had to be Scotty.

"Why should I need a sleeping bag?" I asked. "Has something happened to the hotel in Waboden?"

"Oh there is a good hotel there all right, but we're not there and there is no guarantee that we will be there by tonight. The moose are taking their spring migration. On the way out we had to wait for over a day while a herd crossed the line."

Fortunately, members of the staff at Hudson's Bay house had enlightened me on some of the interesting aspects of the trip I was now taking. I knew that moose crossing the tracks sometimes did hold up the train. Also, I was told this migration usually happened in the fall and north of Waboden.

"So what?" I shrugged as I spoke. "I'll just pull on my parka, use my overcoat for a blanket and curl up on the seat."

"Oh he'll turn out to be a real man of the north."

A third member of the group decided it was his turn to take over the ribbing: "But it will take time — as long as he doesn't give up his fancy shoes for moccasins before he learns to chop wood without losing any toes."

Obviously, to him at least, I appeared to be a real city slicker and not the misplaced farmboy I actually was.

"Why do I need to learn to chop wood?" I asked.

"The stoves here don't run on electricity. They run on fire and the fire has to be fed with wood." As an afterthought he added, "And wood of the right length don't grow on trees."

A man wearing a cap with "news agent" printed across the front approached. "You wanna eat?" he asked each member of the group.

Each of my companions replied in the affirmative and handed the news agent a dollar. I followed their example. A full-course meal in Winnipeg could be bought for thirty-five cents; a dollar could have purchased a smorgasbord banquet. I anticipated a good lunch.

When the news agent left I asked my companions how many choices the menu provided.

"There ain't no menu," John decided to answer my question. "Still, you have a choice. You can eat it or you can leave it. As long as the old boy's got your buck, he don't care."

"But dinna worry lad," Scotty hurried to reassure me. "He cooks up pretty good hash for the price."

A take-what-you-get meal for a dollar meant only one thing — I had left the depression behind and caught up with inflation.

As the train chugged along it seemed that even a shack beside the tracks comprised a settlement large enough to justify a stop. The number of paying customers remained relatively constant. If we lost a passenger at one stop, we gained another passenger at the next stop. At one stop, a clergyman boarded the train. He wore a parka fashioned from beautiful brown fur. Two stops later, after he alighted, I asked John what type of fur was used in the garment.

"That is unborn caribou," he explained. "It's a real good parka but mighty hard to come by. The deer hunting season ain't exactly when they're carrying fully formed young ones."

I considered it odd that a member of the clergy would be flagrantly breaking the law. "Do parsons have special privileges?" I asked.

"No," came the reply. "However, Indians are allowed to kill an animal at any time if they can prove they are starving, and Indians are always starving." As an afterthought he added: "The parka is likely a gift from his congregation."

At six o'clock that evening the Muskeg Express made one of its many halts. No train personnel made any announcement but everyone began to alight. John looked at his watch. "Come on," he said. "It is supper time."

We joined the line of people trooping into a log building where an unlighted sign with the word "Cafe" hung over the door. A gasoline lantern hung from the ceiling, supplying the inside with light. This provided ample illumination for the tables in the center of the room. However, the corner where John and I sat left much to be desired in terms of lighting. A handwritten menu lay in the center of each table. John struck a match on the bottom of the seat of the kitchen-type chair and held the flame so we could see the menu to make our selections. It listed a choice of stew or sausages.

The train crew was first in line and, consequently, occupied the well-lit location in the middle of the room. One member of the crew made the most of his center-stage location.

"I'll take the saucy Jesus," he informed the pretty, teenage Metis waitress. He voiced his order loud enough for people who stood outside to hear and laughed even louder at his joke. The girl responded with a shy giggle. His face reflected his satisfaction with his abilities as a comedian.

After the crew members finished gulping their food and relaxing with an after-dinner cigarette, the untimed and unannounced stop ended. Without so much as one "all aboard," we again entered the coach. The train continued on its way, but at about ten o'clock we stopped.

Before any of my fellow passengers alighted, the local Hudson's Bay Company post manager and the station agent boarded the train. "You better come sit a spell with the wife and me before going to the hotel," said the post manager without introducing himself.

I explained I expected to continue on to Gillam.

"All in good time," he replied. "I booked a room for you in the hotel and the train stops here overnight."

I realized we had reached Waboden.

My free time from the training school gave me a much-dreamed-of opportunity to explore Winnipeg. During one of these exploration trips, the hard-sell line of the proprietor of a secondhand store succeeded in making me the proud owner of a slightly used parka. I took advantage of the overnight stop in Waboden to unpack this bargain.

The next morning I boarded the train wearing a garment more in keeping with those my traveling companions wore. However, the zippered front and the heavy flannel lining still marked me as a tenderfoot. A fair percentage of the coach's ever-changing passenger list broke the monotony of the trip by half-spoofing and half-enlightening the greenhorn (namely me).

By three thirty that afternoon, we arrived at Gillam. The on-again, off-again spoofing raised my temper to the boiling point. I felt that once I left the train I would leave that part of my initiation behind and begin a proper initiation into the art of fur trading. I picked up my bags and hurried from the train.

As I approached the Hudson's Bay store, a slightly built man, who I later learned was the local school teacher, said something to the Gillam post manager, pointed at me and laughed. I dropped my bags and started toward them.

For some reason the school teacher suddenly decided he had business elsewhere. I altered my direction to follow him.

"I'll take you over and introduce you later, Bill. In the meantime we'd better get you lodged in the hotel," said the post manager as he knocked the chip off my shoulder.

I returned to my bags, picked them up and accompanied the manager to the store. The incident was ignored and forgotten.

Planners for the Hudson's Bay railway located the overhaul shops at Gillam. The shops were equipped with two conveniences that most northern communities lacked — electricity and running water. The steam-powered generators provided sufficient power for all the businesses and some of the residences to use incandescent lights. Running water could be found in the hotel, station, railway staff houses and several privately owned houses, including the Hudson's Bay dwelling. However, the majority of the residential area still relied on outdoor plumbing, a water bucket and kerosene lamps.

I learned that my stay in the north's luxury center would last for one week. This stay allowed little more than sufficient time for Henry Mann, the post manager, to give me some much-needed counselling and ensure I was properly outfitted for dog-team travel.

The local natives provided the store with an excellent supply of moccasins, mitts, duffle linings and snowshoes. My credit rating was also excellent. Within half an hour of my arrival I had fulfilled my lifelong dream — I bought a pair of big, duffle-lined, gauntlet mitts. Snowshoes proved to be a painless acquisition. From his stock, Henry selected the pair that he considered best suited to my needs. He then prepared a voucher which transferred the costs to the York Factory post.

Snow goggles of various shapes, sizes and lens colors filled half a shelf in a display case. I was advised to choose a pair with wind protectors at the sides because the wind can blind as effectively as the sun.

On several occasions, other customers interrupted my outfitting endeavor. One time, some Indians arrived to trade. Since the natives only spoke the Cree tongue, I listened intently and soon picked up my first Cree word, *keyabitch,* which means more. The natives frequently used this word. Apparently they not only wanted more money for their furs, they also wanted more credit.

While Henry was busy trading with the natives, a railway employee dropped in to buy tobacco and pass the time of day. He threw out the teasing statement that before I could become a real man of the north I would have to sleep with a squaw and shoot a polar bear. In order to see the reaction his words of advice produced, I looked at the Indian women in the store. Apparently, they did not hear the statement or they did not understand what they heard. I gave him a noncommittal shrug of my shoulders.

Henry suggested I should get the feel of the snowhsoes before I began the trek to York Factory. He lent me his shotgun and directed me to the tree-covered river banks to look for rabbits. Time was of no object and I had no fixed destination. Consequently, I could ease the bite of the thongs or eliminate any build-up of snow underfoot if I simply found one of the well-used paths and removed the snowshoes. I found that the heavy shotgun hampered my efforts to become a self-taught snowshoeing expert. Before I made my second safari I went further into debt at the company store. I armed myself with a twenty-two-caliber rifle, but even that four dollar purchase proved to be excess baggage because I failed to see any game.

As well as scrambling through the bush on snowshoes, I spent a fair amount of time in the store. The time spent gave me an introduction to trading with the Cree Indians.

Like a pre-school child I asked a multitude of questions. I soon had a reason for the frequent use of *keyabitch.* The Cree's social status was a direct relationship to the amount of credit he could obtain from the company store. A trading session could never be considered finalized until the native made at least three requests for a larger amount of credit. Despite such credit requests, bad debts were a rarity. Records of each trapper's past performance were kept, making it difficult for him to receive an advance beyond his ability to repay.

Like the hotel at The Pas, the Gillam hostelry rented rooms without locks on the doors. After I spent four hours during the afternoon looking for rabbits I retired early. Almost immediately, due to the overabundance of fresh air and exercise, I drifted into a sound sleep. Around ten thirty Duke, the rival trader, and another chap rudely awakened me. They threw the blankets over the end of the bed and bodily lifted me. They then stood back and laughed.

"We're having a party at my house," Duke's companion explained "so we decided to drop over and get you to join us."

Since the invitation was as genuine as it was abrupt, I dressed and accompanied them to the scene of the festivities.

At least once during the winter months a moccasin dance took place in the skating rink back home. Before I'd spent five minutes at the Gillam function I realized the home-town effort was a poor imitation of the real thing. A native fiddler provided an alternate source of music to that which a spring-powered gramaphone produced. His rhythm was perfect, but his melody offered little competition to the recorded sound.

One of the training school instructors went to great lengths to warn us about the native girls. He explained we would be reluctant to approach them closer than a distance of ten feet at first. After six months to a year, however, the belle of the village would appear and "WOW." There were two semi-native girls at that dance whom I felt reduced the minimum waiting time the instructor suggested by five months, four weeks and two days. Henry explained to me the next morning that the native women soon change with age. I could not argue with that statement. Who doesn't change?

The partygoers, however, were completely free from racial prejudice. The crowd, comprised of English, Scandinavian, Ukranian and Cree, along with various combinations of all four, freely inter-mingled and immensely enjoyed itself.

We exhausted our supply of refreshments long before we exhausted our energies dancing. Dancing ceased while a collection was taken to purchase another keg of beer. Fortunately, I still had a dollar left from my traveling expense money. I felt no apprehension about throwing my last buck into the hat. I had an excellent credit rating at the Hudson's Bay store.

The following morning the railway worker who gave me the tongue-in-cheek advice about squaws and polar bears, returned to replenish his supply of tobacco.

"I hear you were at the party last night," he said. "What do you think of our blueberry blondes?"

I looked at the case of rifles. "What caliber is best for shooting polar bears?" I asked.

Judging by his expression, I realized he expected a different reply.

Life at Gillam was an enjoyable and an interesting introduction to life in the north. The time passed so quickly I had the feeling I was living in an enchanted land where a day was crowded into ten hours and far less than seven days comprised a week.

Exactly on time, according to the verbal schedule Henry gave me, a dog team arrived from York Factory. Four generations of a Metis family hauled freight for the York Factory post to make their living. The two drivers for this particular team consisted of a father and son combination. The son represented the fifth generation of these freighters.

The father, Jim, stood approximately five foot eleven in his moccasin feet. The collared black sweater he wore closely hugged his body and made it apparent that his chest measurement exceeded his waist measurement by at least a foot. When he bent his arm the sweater sleeve indicated it covered a well-formed biceps. His face was wrinkled in lines which spelled friendship and his eyes twinkled with kindness. Apparently, his above-average strength was balanced with a gentle disposition.

The son, John, was a stripling of approximately fourteen years. His physique already showed it would grow to rival that of his father. Lines were not yet etched into his face, but his face gave every indication he inherited his father's disposition.

The restaurant in the hotel opened at six o'clock and provided me with a breakfast fit for a man about to hit the snowshoe trail. Henry was at the store to make certain I left with all the necessary equipment. He furnished me with a tin plate, porcelain mug, eating utensils and a few words of encouragement. Then I was on my way.

The first twenty miles of the route followed the smooth roadbed of the Hudson's Bay railway. The snow between the rails made an ideal track for the heavily loaded toboggan. However, even the excellent sledding produced a pace far slower than the one I anticipated. My education in dog-team travel had been obtained from watching movies. The team and driver with whom I was traveling had never watched any movies. Their learning came strictly from experience. Their lack of formal training became evident almost as soon as we started the journey. Instead of sitting on the load and skimming over the snow at speeds of twenty to thirty miles per hour, we walked. Consequently, even though Jim constantly urged his dogs to put forth greater effort, the best they could manage was four miles per hour; our average fell below three miles. Within half an hour I learned my second Cree expression, *Ah Tug Eye*. When I asked for a literal translation John looked at me and laughed. Later, after I became more familiar with the language, I realized the expression referred to the south end of a northbound dog.

After traveling for approximately four hours and covering a little better than ten miles we stopped for lunch. Lunch on the trail did not constitute a brief stop at a wayside coffee shop. Instead, firewood had to be gathered and snow had to be melted to make water for tea. The main dish on the menu had to be thawed and then cooked. At this stop, the main dish was bacon and beans. Jim carved some bacon off a frozen slab with a butcher knife, opened a can of beans with the same knife and dumped the food into a cast iron frying pan. If that frying pan had ever been introduced to soap and water it must have been an extremely fast hello. After the mess was cooked, the knife served as a ladle to apportion my ration onto my tin plate. The father and the son sat down with the frying pan between them and passed the butcher knife back and forth. Each alternately helped himself to a bladeful of beans. The menu, table setting and bean balancing act of my companions may not have been acceptable banquet standards, but I have never enjoyed food more.

After the butcher knife lifted the last bean from the frying pan, Jim filled and lit his pipe and placed the unwashed dishes in the grub box. The midday meal was finished and I once more found myself an active member of a freight-hauling crew.

After another four hours of travel we arrived at an empty one-roomed building. On each end of the structure, the word "Amery" appeared in big white letters. When the government first approved the plans for the Hudson's Bay railway it located the northern terminus at Port Nelson. After the roadbed was completed and a huge bridgelike structure extended half a mile into Hudson Bay, the government took a second look at Port Nelson and changed its mind. Gillam was where it took the second look and Amery was where it changed its mind. At Amery the twin lines of steel turned north and ended at the mouth of the Churchill River.

In addition to marking the site of the government's change of mind, Amery Station served a much more functional role. It provided an excellent camping spot for dog-team travelers and a sheltered lunch spot for section men. Apparently, train crews grew a little careless as the engine chugged around the curve that changed its direction from east to north. Frequently, a few lumps of coal fell from the tender but the chance of an unsightly mess building up from these spills was extremely slight. Almost everyone who stopped at Amery immediately checked along both sides of the track. If they happened to notice any black and shiny litter they picked it up and carried it to the building. The potbellied stove that stood in the center of the floor functioned well as a disposal unit for this type of garbage.

Jim followed the established practice of using the camping facilities at Amery for our overnight stop. Before all the dogs stretched out for a rest he began a scouting trip along the tracks. He soon returned grinning from ear to ear and carrying two good-sized lumps of coal. Sleeping beside a stove that continued to produce warmth all through the night was a luxury he seldom enjoyed.

John headed into the bush with a hatchet because he knew that, regardless of the outcome of his father's search for the diamond's poor relation, dry sticks would be required for kindling. By the time his dad returned, John already had the stove changing the atmosphere of the building from icy chill to comfortable warmth.

The dogs were unharnessed, tethered and left to rest. Jim brought in a five-gallon kettle filled with snow and placed the utensil on top of the heater. Each member of the dog team was soon apportioned its share of cornmeal mash. Cooking for the dogs took precedence over cooking for the men.

A sleeping bag without any form of padding between it and a wooden floor is certainly harder than the conventional bed with a boxspring and mattress. Normally, such an abrupt change in sleeping accomodation would have caused me to toss and turn all night. However, the exercise, fresh air and warm room after the cold outside combined to allow me to bed down at eight o'clock and become lost in a deep slumber five minutes later. The obligation to rise at six o'clock the next morning in order to hit the trail came all too quickly. Since I awoke without any telltale bruises, my tossing and turning was minimal.

We continued our journey along the now trackless railroad bed which led to Port Nelson. Originally, the causeway was free from any form of growth. However, due to a lack of maintenance for several years, scrub willow and dwarf evergreen gained a foothold. This growth meant the wind could no longer blow the excess snow from the trail and the resulting depth made snowshoes mandatory.

My rabbit-hunting sorties at Gillam enabled the soles of my feet to become acquainted with snowshoe thongs. This acquaintance certainly did not result in an instant friendship. These non-compulsory snowshoe sorties caused a few blisters to form on the soles of my feet. On this day, however, nature provided us with a slight preview of the spring thaw. The warmer weather caused snowballs to form and to turn to ice right underneath my not-quite-healed blisters. Jim showed me the approved method of clearing the snow from the snowshoes. By giving the edge of the snowshoe a sharp rap with a stick he easily jarred all the snow loose from the thongs. It looked easy and I tried it, but it did not work for me. I found it necessary to use the stick like a scraper in order to clear the snow from the thongs. Whenever I attempted to push ahead and ignore the buildup of snow, the pressure on the balls of my feet caused me to stop and repeat the clearing routine. This procedure added little in the way of enjoyment to my first cross-country hike on snowshoes.

That night I found myself introduced to wilderness camping. The trees of the dwarf forest formed the only shelter from the cool Manitoba breeze which gently wafted in from Hudson Bay. The breeze had little trouble finding numerous openings in this natural shelter. To provide an additional windbreak, Jim built a wall from spruce boughs. He also spread a layer of boughs to serve as a mattress and to insulate the three sleeping bags from the snow-covered ground. While the temperature dropped to twenty degrees below zero Fahrenheit during the night, not even a hint of an icy blast interrupted my sleep. When I awoke the next morning I found I was adding my own sweaty stench to the lining of the well-used eiderdown sleeping bag. The bag formed part of the York Factory post equipment and although I am certain many names appeared before mine on the list of apprentices to use it, it still functioned as well as the day it was new.

The following morning I dressed in light socks, oxfords and overshoes instead of the conventional duffle, heavy socks and moccasins. The cooler day eliminated the problem of icy snow adhering to the snowshoe thongs. The heavy-soled oxfords prevented the thongs from biting into my blistered feet. For the first hour all went well, but I soon began to tire. The inflexible heavy sole prevented my toes from bending. Thus, the front of the snowshoe tipped downward while the back raised well above the surface of the snow with every step. I decided it was better to suffer with the conventional, northern footwear and I decided to change into my moccasins when we stopped for lunch. As if to impress on me the foolishness of attempting to improve on an established custom, Jim failed to call a luncheon break even though twelve o'clock noon came and passed.

At one thirty I learned the reason for a delayed lunch because we arrived at a log cabin. This one-roomed shelter housed an Indian, his wife and two children. In the centre of the structure was an oil drum, converted into a wood heater that radiated warmth. At a distance of three to five feet from this stove, the room felt comfortable. However, if one ventured closer, the smell of scorched clothes warned him to move back. If he moved too far away, the chilling draft which eased through the cracks in the log wall made itself unpleasantly evident.

The top of the stove made an excellent heat source for Jim to cook the usual ration of beans. Instead of using a spoon I decided to sponge up the juice that came with my portion with a slice of bread and butter. Every time the door through which fuel was fed to the stove opened ashes spilled on the floor. Obviously no one bothered to clean them up. Loose hair and pieces of freshly-skinned rabbit added to the mess. I dropped a piece of frozen butter into this pile of refuse. The Indian pounced on it, looked at me and said something in Cree. "Do you want to eat that?" Jim translated.

Before I finished shaking my head, the native scraped off whatever ash and fur he could without losing any of the butter. He took a nibble, smacked his lips and then rushed to share the delicacy with his family. I cut a ten-cent slab from the dollar-per-pound spread and handed it to him. He smiled his thanks and this time took a good third for himself before he passed the remainder along to his wife and family. While we ate the balance of the meal the hungry natives stared at us like begging dogs. However, we finished our lunch without throwing them any further tidbits.

Long before we arrived at the log cabin, the pain from my cold toes reinforced my decision to revert to conventional snowshoe footwear. While Jim repacked the unwashed dishes and lit his pipe I changed back to my moccasins. To provide extra padding for my blistered feet, I folded two handkerchiefs and placed them under the heavy socks. After we resumed our journey, for the first few hundred yards my feet felt as if I had found the solution to snowshoe thong bites. I then discovered I could not permanently eliminate this problem by merely adding a little extra padding.

The toboggan trail along the abandoned railway became progressively worse. The need to break trail further restricted our rate of progress. For me, the phrase "breaking trail" conjured up visions of adventure, but my visions were soon shattered. Breaking trail consisted of preceding the dogs and attempting to flatten a path in the soft snow. Although I lumbered along on my snowshoes ahead of the dogs, John did most of the trailbreaking. He would go ahead for a distance of about 100 yards and mark one edge of the path as he went. He marked the other edge of the path when he returned. After he reached the team, he again turned and stamped down the center portion. Although John traveled the distance three times to my once, he did not find the pace tiring. However, even with a pathway created by four sets of snowshoe tracks and Jim's constant urging, the dogs could barely manage a pace of two miles per hour.

The occasional abandoned set of wagon wheels, a wheelbarrow or some other relic of earth-moving equipment gave us the only evidence we were traveling over a once well-graded railroad bed. By late afternoon, these signs disappeared as our route threaded its way through denser bush. Obviously, Jim decided to follow the government's example and abandon the road to Port Nelson. That night a high creek bank provided us with a sheltered camp site.

After breaking camp the next morning we followed the creek bed to its mouth where we could travel over a smooth causeway. We were on the snow-covered ice of the Nelson River and no trail was visible. Even the well-marked pathway my companions must have made on their way to Gillam could no longer be seen. Some trail breaking still had to be done, but one trip for John as I lumbered along beside him proved sufficient. Actually, we were traveling over a pathway of well-packed snow. A tilting snowshoe made it obvious whenever I stepped too close to the edge.

The river was wide and we traveled close to the northern edge. Although the height of the edge of the river provided little protection from the northern wind, our nearness to the creek edge enabled Jim to select an ideal spot for lunch. He drove his team into a sheltered cove formed at the mouth of a creek.

During the course of the meal, a whisky jack (Canada jay) flew into a nearby pine and began to scold us at great length. I picked up my rifle and started to take aim. Immediately, I was advised to save my ammunition until a more edible target presented itself. My guides explained that although Indians ate whisky jacks when they were properly cooked, time on the trail did not permit proper cooking. In order to cook a whisky jack, it must be boiled. A stone is placed in the same pot and when the stone is soft enough for a knife to cut it, the whisky jack is ready to eat. After watching Jim dexterously use his knife to ladle, spear or sever whenever he found such an operation necessary, it seemed conceivable that he could easily slice a well-boiled stone.

When we made our third overnight wilderness camp, I began telling my companions about the homemade snow planes I had seen. All these planes had the same basic design and they were powered with an automobile engine which drove a push propellor. The complete assembly, which included an enclosed seating arrangement, was mounted on skis. The resulting "go machine" was capable of traveling up to thirty miles per hour.

My daydreaming aloud did not fall on deaf ears. However, my companions showed more concern than interest. I got the impression, possibly due to snowshoe fatigue, they felt they had a slightly weird tenderfoot on their hands. John tried to encourage me when he said we would soon be there. I attempted to obtain his estimate of the number of miles still to be traveled, but he did not understand. I tried another approach and asked how many more sleeps. He replied: "Not many."

He then abandoned all efforts at psychological motivation and began chatting in Cree with his father.

Finally, we arrived at a campsite where Jim elected to spend the final night of our journey. On the south side of the mouth of the Nelson River, three branches of a Metis family had erected a three-cabin settlement. We passed the night in one of these cabins. The factory-finished, top-quality doors, windows and frames which were fitted into these log structures provided the ultimate contrast between modern and old building techniques.

I later learned when Port Nelson was first abandoned that anyone who had access to the deserted site on the north bank of the Nelson River and had a bit of skill in dismantling had no difficulty obtaining whatever building necessities he required. A good chinking job sealed the cracks between the logs so well I was unable to detect even the slightest draft from any portion of the room. The floor, fashioned from split logs, gave every indication of being freshly washed as even the wood, bleached from frequent scrubbings, around the stove was spotless. Although the structure was of sufficient size to contain two large rooms, no attempt to erect a partition had been made. The man of the house explained that, since they had a far better home residence at York Factory, they used this campsite only during the trapping season.

We enjoyed a leisurely breakfast and did not break camp until after eight o'clock. While I was tying on my snowshoes, John explained we were almost to our destination and we only stopped for the night in order to enable me to rest my blistered feet. I later learned that a nearly exhausted dog team was the prime reason for our overnight stop. Jim feared that if the post manager considered the team's performance did not measure up, the hauling contracts would be given to another trapper. Jim had no cause for alarm, however, because he owned the only readily available team at York Factory.

By the time we arrived I was able to translate John's "nearly there" into two or three more overnight stops; and "almost there" into a couple of meal stops.

For some reason the need to continually push both dog and man no longer existed. Around ten thirty we stopped for the first coffee break we had taken on the trip. Jim boiled his kettle and made tea. The break took longer than Jim usually allowed for our noon stop.

Shortly after we resumed travel, John pointed to a break in the trees where a huge white structure topped with a lookout tower stood clearly visible. "*Kitchie Waskahagan,*" he said, which means big white house.

I made him repeat the phrase several times until I mastered the pronunciation. I now had a vocabulary of three Cree expressions and I felt free to use two of them anywhere and anytime.

Suddenly, I noticed we were on a well-traveled trail. Jim urged his dogs, which were still rested after our coffee break, into a fast trot. I found it necessary to kick off my snowshoes and run in order to keep up. We passed what I later learned was the school house, together with several other log structures. We stopped in front of a frame dwelling. Jim waited until I caught my breath before he took me inside where I received an introduction to Archdeacon Faries and his wife. Mrs. Faries immediately told me about the church service held every Sunday morning for the English-speaking residents of the post. She concluded her enthusiastic description with the thought that she hoped I would attend. I began to reply that since my parents were of the Anglican faith, I would certainly feel at home at the service. However, the archdeacon interrupted to chide his wife for attempting to extract a promise from me.

After a short visit, we proceeded to the store. Harold Bland, the post manager, stood with his back soaking up the warmth from an oil barrel heater. His hands rested on his hips and a straight-stemmed pipe protruded from one corner of his mouth. The bowl of the pipe was empty and upside down.

I introduced myself and explained I had arrived to help or to bug him as time alone would prove. Before he either spoke or proffered his hand, he spent a good two minutes visually scrutinizing me. His steady gaze began at my head, descended to my feet and returned to my head. I matched him stare for stare, my own hands dangling loosely at my sides.

After the staring match ended in a draw, Harold took my hand and initiated a squeezing match. Milking cows and doing other farm chores, combined with the use of the exercising equipment at the Parish Hall Gym, enabled me to develop a powerful grip. This match lasted no more than five seconds before he decided our get-acquainted ceremonies were completed. The time arrived for me to meet the rest of the Bland family and to be shown around the post.

Historic York Factory

York Factory is filled with history. It changed hands seven times while the French and the English vied with each other to see who would wrest Canada from the Indians. Finally the French won and sailed away, leaving the English to fight the mosquitoes and battle for a foothold in the muskeg.

This historic past immediately started to manifest itself. Harold picked up a key about four times as large as any I had previously seen. He used it to fasten an enormous lock which secured a door approximately four by eight feet and three inches thick. Obviously, over a hundred years previously the Hudson's Bay Company decided it was at York Factory to stay. The Company constructed a building solid enough to serve its needs for the next several centuries.

We left the store and walked to Harold's house where he introduced me to his Cree Indian wife and those of his seven children who had not yet started school. Mrs. Bland showed no hesitation as she grasped my hand. Although she only spoke the word, "hello," her broad smile conveyed an unreserved welcome.

She spoke to her husband in Cree. Not once did she use any of the three phrases I had already learned. Consequently, even though I listened intently, I failed to understand even one word. As soon as she finished speaking, Harold showed me to my room.

I sat on the edge of the bed. Finally, I was able to change into footwear which was firm enough to prevent the soles of my feet from demanding attention at every step. I removed the moosehide moccasins, the duffle linings and the two pairs of heavy socks. When I finally peeled off the improvised pads, made from hankies, half the skin from my blistered soles peeled with them. Two freshly laundered handkerchiefs served as bandages which I placed over the sores on my feet. A clean pair of socks held them in place. I eased my feet into my oxfords and I took a couple of steps. I found I could now walk without being constantly reminded my feet were damaged. A quick glance in the mirror reminded me I was in need of a good wash and a shave.

I returned to the kitchen in search of water. My arrival in the kitchen coincided with the arrival of the remainder of the Bland children, all of whom came home for their lunch break. Two of them were girls in their mid-teens. I had heard rumors teenaged half-breed girls were attractive and these two supported that rumor to the point that I didn't know if I got hot water or ice water for shaving.

The seating arrangement at the table reflected Harold Bland's interpretation of family hierarchy. Sons were given a higher status than daughters and after the initial grading, age seniority formed the basis for a second inflexible rating. Mrs. Bland, on the other hand, showed no traces of partiality toward any of her children. She considered all her children to be of equal status and equal importance.

As soon as lunch was completed, a work routine commenced and Harold and I returned to the store. Perhaps one hundred years earlier when the structure was first completed, the word *store* was a more apt description. Now, however, only a small portion of the building served for retail purposes. Ninety per cent of the balance of the huge two-and-one-half-story structure stood empty. We paused in the room, approximately twenty-five by thirty feet, which was reserved for bartering, only for the few moments required to stoke up the oil drum heater and ensure the massive door was securely locked. The ever-hungry natives would not leave home with the intention of stealing a good feed. Nevertheless, it was poor policy to tempt them with easy access to an unattended store.

Our predecessors were well aware that the river flowed in a direction bearing slightly to the north. However, one practice probably established several centuries earlier ignored correct compass directions. This practice still prevailed and both natives and Metis referred to the river as if it flowed in a straight line to the east. The northern river bank formed the southern boundary of the settlement. This locally established set of directions placed the space allotted for dealing with shoppers in the northwest corner of the building.

Although the little up-to-date shop was a carbon copy of the general store which could be found in any small prairie town, stepping into the remainder of the warehouse complex was like stepping into a past century. I followed Harold along a wide hallway as he began to conduct a guided tour of the structure.

We passed along the corridor to the store office where Harold proudly showed me a cribbage board he had fashioned from a walrus tusk. The pegging surface was embossed with etchings of deer and other forms of wildlife while the base of the triangular shaped tusk served as a storage space for pegs. While Harold felt proud of the artistry displayed on the face of the cribbage board, his pride and joy was a two-foot-square piece of hardwood. He had half-finished outlining a moose on this wood. At the sight of the partially finished plaque, he completely forgot the purpose at hand. He picked up a nearby hammer and nail and resumed working at his hobby. As he tapped the nail just heavily enough to barely puncture the wood, he continued to make the series of embedded dots which outlined the animal and the background foliage. He spent a full fifteen minutes engrossed in his creative pastime before my restlessness caused him to remember my presence and my need to be introduced to the York Factory surroundings.

We retraced our footsteps along the corridor. About halfway to the store, Harold opened a door which led to an inner courtyard. There seemed to be no explanation as to why the open space existed in the center of the structure, but it did provide an excellent vantage point from which to assess the enormous size of the complex. Four separate wings formed the walls of this square. Three of these wings stood two stories high while the wing to the south boasted a third story and a lookout tower. This higher, southern wing ensured the lower portion of the square would be completely shaded from sunlight, even during mid-summer. This inner courtyard, now covered with snow, had sides which measured close to fifty feet long. A set of wooden walks met at right angles in the center of this muskeg patio. These crosswalks linked doors in the center of each wing. Harold explained during the summer the walks were necessary to prevent a person from sinking to his knees in the swamp. My curiosity caused me to do a little investigating on my own during the summer season. I found the walks covered portions of a drainage system which led from the foundations of the building to the river.

We closed the door on the scene which looked as inviting as a picnic site in an open field during a blizzard and followed the corridor beyond the office door until we came to a flight of stairs. Over the years, many hands polished, smoothed and oiled the handrail near the stairs. The friction of feet on the treads marked a pathway slightly off center toward the handrail side. The landing on the second floor immediately led into a huge storeroom where I noticed a few furs piled in one corner. Walls twelve feet high supported massive timbers which in turn supported the gable roof. Posts were fastened with metal braces from the center of the crossbeams to the peak of the gables. No sags and no other signs of wear were visible. This building was an example of post-and-beam construction at its ultimate. The construction resulted in a roof without wavers and walls without warps.

In addition to the massive beams, long lengths of knot-free boards were used in the construction of the big white house. Available records indicated the structure was virtually completed before 1840. The trees in the forest of runt evergreens which I passed through on my way from

Gillam were incapable of supplying timber of either the quality or the dimensions of that used in the building. It appeared transporting special material to the site of an important project was an accomplished process early in the nineteenth century.

In the center of the storeroom I saw a huge fur press. My first quick glance caused me to wonder if I was looking at an instrument from a medieval torture chamber. When I compared the size and the quality of the beams used to fashion the baling device with those used in the building, the building beams were obviously second best. The metal turnscrew and the reinforced corners gave the impression the machine was also built to last for centuries. I later learned that the baling press beams were fashioned from timber cut in India. Harold remarked we would be baling fur after Easter. Enough fur was already collected for a couple of small bales. I crossed over to the pile and took a closer look. He was right — the enormous size of the room dwarfed the size of the stock of fur.

We proceeded to the north end of the structure where another storeroom stretched the full length of the building. Since the heavy crossbeams eliminated the need for center posts, a cleared floor area twenty-six by 105 feet existed. With the exception of a discarded rug which Mrs. Bland had found too difficult to keep clean with her primitive housekeeping equipment, the room was empty. Thirteen windows along the north wall, two at each end with several more looking into the inner court, provided ample light to observe the dust which had collected over the years.

We gave no more than a passing glance to the two empty rooms that comprised the entire second story of the east wing. We then entered the section that overlooked the Hayes River. The layout, combined with the markings in this storage area, showed it had been a dry goods warehouse for generations. Tiers of shelves reaching from the floor to the ceiling were so closely placed, the aisles between them allowed barely sufficient room to walk. Markings such as blankets, yard goods or men's underwear, ensured every item was shelved in its proper section. The empty rows of shelves clearly showed the laws of supply and demand were already in existence despite the fact that the days of computerized merchandising had yet to arrive.

Only a small supply of the few items which could be readily sold were stocked. A few pairs of men's socks, men's underwear, men's work shirts and trousers seemed to comprise the entire stock of ready-to-wear garments. Several cubicles which contained bolts of cloth, yarn, knitting needles and sewing accessories provided do-it-yourself kits for women's apparel. A few bolts of brightly colored print were the most noticeable objects in these cubicles. Harold explained these bolts were kept from the native's view until Easter. If the goods were placed on display during midsummer when they first arrived, the native women would cajole their husbands into attempting to obtain them on credit. Although the Hudson's Bay Company extended credit according to each individual trapper's success, this credit enabled the native to obtain his trapline necessities. Removing the temptation eliminated the need to refuse. Also, since only one shipment arrived each year, the spring and the summer stocks were not displayed before the weather showed some promise that spring was around the corner.

When my dry-goods merchandising lesson in the York Factory style ended, we completed our circuit of the second floor by finding our way into the southern end of the west wing. No clues existed to indicate the room was intended for any particular purpose. An aged and battered pool table stood in what appeared to be the exact center of the chamber showing that it now functioned as a billiard hall. To restore it to usable condition, Harold had stretched a blanket over the playing surface. We stopped long enough to play a game of billiards. This game marked the beginning of my formal instruction in the Cree language. Instead of counting in English, Harold used the *payuk-neesyou-nisto's* (one-two-three's) of the native tongue. These words formed the basis of the Cree-English dictionary I began to compile.

When we finished the billiard game we proceeded up another set of stairs to the third story. The main interest in the empty room was its access to a reversing stairway which led to the lookout tower. The six-sided tower provided an unobstructed view of the surrounding countryside. During the tour Harold informed me that all the interesting relics were taken from York Factory for museum purposes. However, possibly because its outer glass was badly scratched, a powerful telescope remained on one of the window benches. If I rested it on the casing of an open window, I easily discerned details at a distance of fifteen miles. This vantage point also gave an excellent view of the building roof. For some reason the third story was shingled with tin while the roof on the rest of the building was covered with sheet lead. One of the local Metis told me his grandfather once worked on the third story and on the lookout tower. However, he could not remember if the old man talked about working on the two-story section. This discussion seemed to substantiate the local rumor that the third story and the lookout tower were additions. It also left me wondering if the sheet lead salvaged from the original structure was used to roof the lookout tower. But my verbal historian, who was now a great-grandfather in his own right, could not answer my question.

Window benches with hinged lids provided seats for anyone who wished to scan the countryside from the lookout tower. Apparently, these benches also provided a storage space for obsolete records. Most of these papers had been taken to Hudson's Bay House in London for safekeeping, but some loose and damaged pages from the records books still remained. Even though the window benches were comparatively empty, many of these sheets lay scattered on the floor. During my stay at York Factory, I spent many interesting hours browsing through the written transactions which took place many decades earlier. One transaction, dated 1865, showed that a cabin boy received the princely sum of one pound sterling for four months' service and he paid one dollar a pound for plug tobacco. Thankfully, conditions for the worker improved since 1865.

After spending a brief period exploring the relics in the lookout tower we returned to the ground floor. The south wing still had two rooms in use. In a plank bin on the north end of one room, a heap of sawdust covered a few blocks of ice. I could not understand why the need for winter refrigeration existed during the winter in this northern community. I later learned that the bin served as a storage place for wild game. The other room functioned as a storage warehouse for flour, sugar, tea and other grocery items which arrived in bulk.

We followed the empty corridor-like rooms and soon found ourselves at the north end of the building in a room which adjoined the store. This room contained two barrels of salt pork and a shank of ham. Harold had ordered the ham for his Easter feast. Even though the room abutted the heated store, the ham remained solidly frozen until the religious holiday.

We passed through the open archway into the store where I saw sugar, tea, tobacco and other fast-moving items occupied shelf space directly behind the serving counter. We stoked up the drum heater, unlocked the door and returned to the office. The quick tour of the building which we'd just completed took two hours. I found it not only interesting but also educational. A fringe segment of my learning concerned footwear. The cold from the floors penetrated the soles of leather oxfords. I lost no time removing my shoes in order to warm my feet near the office heater.

Until the late 1920s, York Factory's population was large enough to warrant a telephone system. Remnants of the system were still in evidence, but the only portion still in use consisted of a switch fastened on the main door in such a manner that a telephone bell in the office rang whenever anyone entered the store.

Despite the fact we were little more than acquainted, Harold and I already formed the type of comradeship that would permit two men to live together in semi-isolation. We could both remain silent and still enjoy each other's company. We were relaxing in such an atmosphere when the doorbell sounded. We listened and heard footsteps approaching the office. The sound of solid soles as they hit the plank floor indicated our visitor was not a moccasin-clad native. When the person entered, we saw it was the local school master.

The school master's entrance turned the peaceful atmosphere into one of tension. I later learned one of the Bland youngsters was making a poor showing at school and, like a dutiful parent, Harold held the teacher fully responsible for the child's lack of scholastic achievement.

York Factory had a small white settlement and even without a tiff over a schoolboy's accomplishments, the completely different living philosophies of these two men made a personality clash unavoidable.

The school teacher set a fine example for his pupils. He totally abstained from using tobacco and alcohol. Moreover, I never heard him use profanity. Although he rarely lit it, Harold seemed to have a pipe in his hand during most of his waking hours. At York Factory his consumption of alcohol was directly dependent on its availability. When he considered the situation demanded a few descriptive words he proved himself quite willing and able to utter them.

Although Churchill could lay claim to being the birthplace of the Hudson's Bay Company, York Factory could lay claim to being the nursery. In 1681 the first Fort was established in the York Factory area. The ensuing intermingling between Europeans and Cree Indians resulted in a large Metis population. For several centuries, members of this half-breed colony were loyal servants of the Hudson's Bay Company but now Harold and myself were the only servants on the payroll. However, at least half a dozen of these Metis families remained. All were former employees from families to whom the Hudson's Bay Company had seen fit to award generations of loyal service by setting up a trust fund. From this trust fund they were permitted to draw a certain amount each month for provisions. The morning after my arrival one female member from each of these families came into the store. The money they received from the fund enabled them to purchase one small article such as a pound of tea, a pound of sugar or a pound of lard. At the same time, they could make a firsthand assessment of the new *ogamassis*, or little boss.

In place of topcoats, these women wore shawls or scarves wrapped around their heads and shoulders. All the women wore dresses made from colored print or gingham. A quick glance at their feet indicated they compensated for the light material used in the dresses with several flannel petticoats. Although all the garments were ankle length, the dresses appeared about one half inch shorter than the undergarments. This appearance was possibly due to the extra padding from the underclothing which caused the outer garments to ride higher. Whatever the reason, the petticoats hung in layers like shingles on a roof.

The builders of the 1830s excelled in erecting structures which were sturdy enough to last several centuries. The builders did not, however, excel in building weatherproof quarters. The outside temperature dropped no lower than that to which I was acclimatized. Inside the store, however, the floor felt like the ceiling of an uninsulated refrigeration plant. This coldness was at least partially due to the fact that, in order to withstand the heaving that the frozen muskeg caused, the floor floated on separate footings free from the walls. By noon of my second day I was forced to revert to my moccasins and three pairs of socks in order to withstand the cold which eased up through the floor.

Harold was born in England and he migrated to Canada while still a young man. Shortly after his arrival he signed on with the Hudson's Bay Company. Now, after more than twenty-five years and over half his life, he still maintained many of his English customs in his adopted country. Tea time was announced every afternoon around three thirty or four o'clock by one of his children arriving at the store with two cups of tea. No matter how carefully the youngster carried the refreshment, some tea splashed from the cup into the saucer by the time it arrived. The empty cup and saucer often would freeze together while they sat on the counter which was little more than twelve feet from the drum heater. I used to feed fuel to that heater until the top of the stove and the bottom of the pipes turned red. However, an open campfire in the great outdoors radiated heat further than that drum heater in the confines of the store.

Records showed the house in which we lived was built around 1840 to serve as a bachelor's quarters. A quick glance at the present condition of the house gave every assurance carpenters had not worked on it since it was erected.

The main floor of the house consisted of a central mess hall with two bedrooms on the west side, one bedroom in the southeast corner, and a pullman-type kitchen in the northeast corner. A stairway with a built-in bookcase formed a portion of its outside wall and backed onto the bedrooms on the west side. Before leaving Winnipeg, I was told of the extensive library which existed at York Factory. However, the few books of fairly recent vintage which occupied space on the stairway shelves did not support that statement. I later learned many volumes, some of which dated back to the early 1870s, were taken to a museum in London. An upright piano filled the balance of the wall space beside the stairway. Although music never occupied a high priority on my list of interests, I could easily tell it was badly out of tune. When, why and how the piano arrived at York Factory could not be confirmed. One rumor hinted that Mrs. Hargreaves, whose husband was the officer in charge of the York Factory operation during the 1840s, brought it from England.

The steep pitch of the roof permitted the attic to be utilized for additional upstairs rooms. The attic consisted of a center hall with long and narrow bedrooms on the east and west ends. Although windows built into the gable ends of the house provided ample light for the bedrooms, a small dormer window inserted in the southern slope of the roof provided the only light for the center hall. If you sat on the floor, it was possible to look through this window towards the river. From a standing position, it was impossible to see beyond the confines of the room. Pictures of the house taken in the early 1900s show this dormer window was not installed before that date. Possibly, some enterprising factor saw fit to move it from an abandoned house to its present location. Records indicate the upstairs portion was used to furnish accommodation for the lower-ranked workers. The lower portion provided accommodation considered more suitable for people who were higher on the company's success ladder.

Like the huge warehouse, the building showed its age. The worn treads on the stairs, the antique furniture with missing hinges and missing drawer pulls, and the worn woodwork around the windows and doors all testified to links with the past.

When York Factory was first established, water was bailed out of the Hayes River. This supply source obviously proved adequate through the centuries since no deviations from the original method had ever been introduced. I inherited the task of carrying water. With a wooden yoke over my shoulders and a ten-gallon kettle suspended from each end, I would struggle up the river bank into the house and pour my load into a barrel near the kitchen stove. As the incoming tide from Hudson Bay flowed inland far beyond the post site, care had to be taken to dip for water only when the river current ensured the water was salt free.

The Bland kitchen with its ample supply of firewood and, I suspect, the occasional cup of tea with canned milk and sugar, made a favorite gathering place for the native and Metis women of the community. Mrs. Bland helped me to compile my English-Cree dictionary. Consequently, she was well aware of the native words I could readily understand. Whenever I dumped a pail of water she would praise the lifting power in my strong arms. Although the remarks were made in Cree to her company, they sufficiently pleased my male vanity to assure her an adequate supply of water.

One afternoon her visitors included a recent mother with a three-day-old baby. Mrs. Bland observed since the infant's eyes were blue like mine, I must certainly be the father. Immediately I replied *moona neena*, or not me.

Something in the way I pronounced the words greatly amused the squaws. They made me repeat the words at least a dozen times and each repetition brought forth fresh bursts of laughter. For the balance of my stay at York Factory, Mrs. Bland and her friends continuously accused me of anything they calculated would bring a *moona neena* reply.

From the day of my arrival at York Factory until the warmer days of spring melted the snow, the house, the store and the way the local inhabitants dressed and lived created a lifestyle that turned back the clock at least fifty years. When the spring thaw exposed the snow-covered relics, I felt like I was stepping from 1839 into 1939 every time I visited the school teacher's quarters and listened to his radio.

Cannon balls were in greater abundance than dandelions in an unkempt lawn. Various areas of the settlement were linked with wooden walks. We improvised a game of bowls as we rolled the cannon balls down the walks. Much to the disgust of the older residents, the roar of cannon balls again echoed throughout the settlement.

During my period of winter confinement at York Factory, I went to the river for water, wandered around the store complex, and every Sunday morning I walked the fifty yards which separated the house from the church. When the pathways, many of which ended where a few relics lay half buried in the muskeg, began to emerge from the snow, I realized the walks which served so well as bowling greens were a necessity. If you took one step beyond their protection, you immediately sank into the muskeg. In such cases, the frozen sub-surface became a blessing.

One of these walkways led in an easterly direction from the

buildings over a wooden bridge and ended at a cemetery. The granite grave markers and the small white picket fences gave every indication this graveyard was once well-maintained. Maintenance now consisted of digging a new grave whenever a bereavement made such a sad task necessary. The lack of upkeep permitted some of the older grave markers to fall over. I yielded to my curiosity and lifted some of these markers to an upright position. When I cleared the writing, I learned this burial place had been in existence since 1830. I later learned these plots were an extension of an earlier cemetery. Possibly in order to use the drier ground which the drainage provided, the original site bordered the river bank. Due to the continual crumbling of the bank, many of these graves and markers fell into the swift-flowing waters of the Hayes River. This new location occupied a slight rise in the ground and eased back from a creek gulley which the wooden bridge spanned. The graves were secured from the crumbling river bank, but already indications existed to show that the burial plots close to the creek bank were beginning to crumble into the creek. The drainage this area enjoyed provided a drier portion of muskeg. Board sidewalks were no longer necessary and dirt paths served in their stead.

The remnants of a powder house shared this desirable location. This house was obviously built to last. Masonry walls thirty inches thick and eight feet high enclosed a rectangle approximately six by eight feet. Although no one I spoke with could remember this structure in its original form, at least two people recalled the reminiscences passed on by their grandparents. These stories established that an egress never existed in the walls. Nature had corrected this oversight seventy-odd years before my arrival when a lightning storm demolished a portion of the south wall. Most of the broken masonry had long since disappeared. Good foundation stones for log cabins are where you find them. Since it was impossible to keep the powder dry without the benefit of a roof, the storehouse certainly was topped in some fashion, but only the solid masonary walls now remained. Solid timbers and lead or tin shingles were also scarce commodities in the community. Like masonry blocks they had a tendency to disappear.

Two rumors existed which pertained to the entrance to this explosives storehouse. One rumor was of a tunnel, but no evidence of a tunnel existed. The other rumor was of a roof hatch, but no physical evidence remained for me to prove or to disprove this theory either. Since the entrance to a destroyed powder house had no direct bearing on my present standard of living, I let my youthful curiosity follow different directions.

Only the use of a canoe for transportation made it possible to observe the relics which the crumbling river bank unearthed. Remains of wooden kegs, portions of boats, the ubiquitous cannon balls, bits of anchor chain, remnants of wooden wheels and even a protruding cannon barrel all gave evidence that this area was a settlement with a historic past.

By following the boardwalks and taking advantage of the solid footing they provided, it was possible to look in every direction and see half-submerged relics jutting from the muskeg. Bits of brick and pieces from some wooden household item or metal tool were so abundant it appeared as if the non-decomposable items from a garbage dump were emptied into the swamp. Only treasures, with no sign of rotting refuse, remained in evidence. On my first sightseeing tour, my mechanical curiosity lured me into stepping off the walk in order to retrieve a metal object that appeared interesting. I barely took three steps before I sank up to my knees in the cold oozing mud. It became obvious why so many interesting relics remained unmolested for years. I followed the example of my predecessors and decided to leave these treasures where they lay.

Two cannon which were sufficiently restored to appear workable stood in front of the store-warehouse complex. A coat of black paint successfully camouflaged the brass barrels. Apparently, the guns were molded before nameplates which gave the date of manufacture were used. But the holes used for firing proved they were not of recent vintage. Portions of a gun carriage were clearly visible half-buried in the muskeg and half-protruding from the creek bank. However, the authentic base remained where it lay and bases fashioned from plank and secured with modern nails supported the barrels in a fixed position. The same black paint which successfully disguised the molded bronze also covered these bases. The local oral history reported that one of these barrels was recovered from the river. Subsequently, the wet fuse was removed and a new one was inserted and lit. The weapon fired. Initially, I considered the story to be entirely the figment of someone's imagination. After I thought about the possibility of waterproof wadding being used to pack the powder and an airtight fuse placed in the firing hole, I decided it might possibly have happened.

Occasionally, a second walk branched from the main path and led to either the foundations of a demolished building or ended abruptly to provide a platform ideally suited for jumping into the ocean of muskeg. Usually, though, only short stubs showing the beginnings of these runners remained. The natives considered the seasoned lumber too valuable to be left in order to provide walkways to nowhere, when it could be used to manufacture tables, benches and other essential furnishings. A picket fence indicated one of these stubs provided the walkway to a family residence. Two massive concrete slabs were the only remains of another building. Broken bits of blue-emblazoned porcelain, sparkling from a heap of ashes at another site, indicated the dwellers in this building preferred china to the more substantial enamel mugs and plates.

Every turn reminded me the settlement in which I lived was once the bustling center of a fur trade empire. But the remains of buildings and the empty buildings scheduled to be dismantled clearly indicated this booming era had passed. The port of Churchill, Hudson's Bay railway and other transportation facilities completely eliminated York Factory's need as a supply depot. The links with history which were now so much in evidence would soon sink into the muskeg. The dwarf forest had already started spreading into the abandoned areas. Nevertheless, the archives in Hudson's Bay house in London and the English, French and Canadian history books will ensure memories of York Factory will continue, even if it is only another name for a school child to remember.

Contemporary York Factory

Some fifty yards northeast of the staff house stood the English church and roughly one mile to the west stood the Cree church. Every Sunday, Archdeacon Faries conducted a morning service in the English church and a midafternoon service in the Cree church. His wife led the singing and she provided the organ accompaniment at both services. These two adult services, combined with Sunday school, ensured the Faries were an extremely busy couple on Sundays.

In the English church, the brass plates attached to the pews and the frames of the stained glass windows ensured all who attended the services were informed how previous officers and families of the Hudson's Bay Company gave more than a token offering on the collection plate. A name plate on the front pew showed a former governor of the Hudson's Bay Company contributed it. Since my position with the company gave me a high social status in the community, I had the privilege of occupying this pew. However, I instead chose to sit in an unmarked pew at the rear of the church. The Bland children and their friends occupied the same pew.

Mrs. Faries lost no time in taking me to task for my choice of seats. Much to her vexation and her husband's obvious approval I replied, "All men are equal in the eyes of the Lord. In this house of worship, all seats should be free and unappropriated."

She assumed I chose the seat merely to sit amid a bevy of pretty girls and to avoid maintaining the dignity which sitting at the front of the congregation would have forced me to maintain. Her assumption was reasonably accurate on both counts, but it did not provide her with sufficient ammunition to refute my arguments.

By scrounging the necessary material and donating their labor, the natives built the Cree church. Contributions from various mission societies combined with assistance from the Hudson's Bay Company supplemented the natives' efforts. The Depression and the dwindling size of the York Factory establishment combined to all but eliminate these forms of assistance. However, the donation socials held at Port Nelson provided far more supplies than the building required to keep it in good repair. A recently installed stained glass window shed its filtered rays on the altar. A belfry, which also showed indications it was a recent acquisition, topped the entrance. Every Sunday afternoon the sound of the bell drifted well beyond the fort limits as the archdeacon summoned his faithful.

I once had the honor of attending a special service inside this church. Following the usual practice, one of the local Metis borrowed a wedding ring from the store. Even though he spoke English when he traded, he enlisted the aid of an interpreter to relay a special request. He wanted me to be the best man at his wedding and I naturally accepted.

The service was conducted entirely in Cree and I found it impossible to follow. However, all went well until I had to change places with the groom. The archdeacon had to revert to English to explain I should step back and let the groom take my place. Whenever we met afterward, he took great pleasure as he reminded me how he almost managed to end my bachelor's freedom.

Special services held in both churches marked the arrival of Easter and reminded all the local residents of its religious significance. However, the Sunday of the first full moon after March twenty-first indicated more than the beginning of a Christian holiday to the York Factory natives. Although they normally ignored clocks and relied on their natural instincts to tell when morning arrived, when night came, and when they should eat, they did live according to the seasons. Easter marked the end of winter hunting and the beginning of muskrat trapping. Easter also meant the time had arrived for people to return to their York Factory homes from their winter camps.

The yard goods that were reserved for the spring season were taken from the storage shelf and placed on the display shelf. Almost immediately, the entire female population aged six to sixty-six came to admire the bright spring colors on display. Besides the few women fortunate enough to be able to draw from a trust fund, only those women whose husbands were successful on the trap line could afford to buy the goods. Ninety per cent of the women could do no more than look longingly. Brightness of color, rather than the texture or the quality of the cloth proved to be the principal selling factor. I am certain that had both been listed at the same price, a piece of brightly colored cotton print would have been chosen over a piece of pure, plain, white silk. Most prints sold for twenty-five cents per yard. (Winnipeg prices listed two or perhaps three yards for the same price.) We paid five cents per squirrel skin and we were unable to place a graded value on many of the muskrat skins greater than a dime. A yard of cloth was the minimum quantity we sold. More than once I barely managed to suppress my desire to pay the difference from my own pocket when a bright-eyed youngster wanted a piece of cloth in exchange for her squirrel or third-rate muskrat skin. There were many bright-eyed youngsters at York Factory. I could not show favoritism and I could not be the great white uncle to them all. Moreover, since Gillam offered the closest competition, the Hudson's Bay Company practically held a monopoly on all fur buying in the area. As a result, the natives experienced little contact with white people. A generous estimate would place no more than forty per cent of the natives having ventured far enough to see the train tracks between Gillam and Churchill. For the balance, the big white house provided their only contact with the business world.

Once Harold felt reasonably certain that all available skins were purchased, he decided to use the special baling press. The furs were carefully segregated, counted and arranged in piles. A square of sacking, sufficient in size to cover the base plate and allow enough overhang to form the sides of the bale, was placed in the correct position in the press. In ascending order of size, the pelts were placed inside the sacking after they had been counted for at least the third time. When Mr. Bland felt satisfied that sufficient fur to form a good-sized bale rested within the working area of the press, he placed a second piece of hessian on top of the heap and gave me the signal to begin slowly twisting the turnscrew. The pressure plate eased down until the heap decreased to a quarter of its previous size.

The bale was then ready for stitching. Harold pushed the baling needle through the top sacking and using the stitches to gain additional pull, he secured the edges to the square he had placed for a cover. After he was satisfied that the stitching would last through the ocean voyage to Hudson's Bay House in London, the pressure was released and the bale removed from the press. I stenciled on the "YF" for York Factory, the bale number and 269. This number 269 signified the fur was baled during that year of the company's operation. Several copies were made of the contents of each bale. One list was placed in a special pocket sewn on the outside of the bale, a second was used as a bill of lading, a third was retained for post records, and a fourth was forwarded to the Nelson River District in Winnipeg.

Like the youngsters and the mothers in the more settled parts of North America, the youngsters in York Factory looked forward to the disappearance of snow. This disappearance marked the commencement of outdoor games. Whenever they could find a ball, youngsters up to approximately the age of fourteen years appeared to prefer ball games. The older children had an all-season pastime which they gave top preference, but during the spring and the early summer they showed an inclination to rank ball games as their second most desirable sport.

Since most of the terrain which surrounded the post consisted of an unadulterated sea of muskeg, I was surprised to learn that an area suitable for a baseball diamond existed. However, this ballpark was originally designated as the woodyard. Over the years, in order to keep the houses and the halls of the settlement warm, vast quantities of firewood were chopped and sawn. In the process, heaps of chips and sawdust were trampled into the quagmire. Moreover, although no relics of machinery remained to support them, rumors were prevalent that a sawmill had also been located on this site. This mill added an additional supply of sawdust to the muskeg fill. The fill, combined with the drainage which proximity to the river provided, resulted in an area suitable for use as a playing field.

An oversized goalpost erected for hanging fish nets marked the southern edge. Willow struggling to derive nourishment from the muskeg bordered the western edge. A boardwalk leading to the school and the archdeacon's residence formed the northern edge of the boundary. A patch of the ubiquitous quagmire prevented the eastern edge from reaching the giant warehouse.

Equipment availability placed limitations on the type of game that could be played. Softball could be played with one ball, one homemade bat, and a group of enthusiastic participants. We played softball. Since I had enjoyed several seasons' experience in this sport, I soon found that, in comparison to the locals, I could excel in any position I chose to play. I also soon found that the game played here had slightly different objectives. Excelling or winning mattered little. Socially mixing, rather than competing, seemed to be the main objective. I did not fully understand all the words used when the players shouted to each other. Still, I understood enough to realize that encouragement was shouted to everyone, teammate and rival alike.

The 1939 baseball season at York Factory lasted only a couple of weeks. Then the youth who owned the ball moved to another location, and naturally he took his sports equipment with him. The bat, carved from a length of green spruce, doubtless found its way into somebody's stove. It remained on the playing field to become the first stick in the logpile that began to build around the first of August. Apparently, experience proved early August to be the ideal time to float rafts of firewood down the river in preparation for winter. The wood could be cut into suitable lengths at some later date.

During the winter, bathing proved to be a major undertaking. It is easy to see how the theory originated that leaving body oil on one's skin helps to withstand the cold. When the ice left the Hayes River in early May, neither the school teacher nor myself could refuse the open invitation to go swimming. I soon ordered a new bathing suit through the mail. Even mail dependent on an outboard-equipped canoe link with a once-a-week train enabled the suit to arrive at York Factory before the river warmed to swimming temperature.

A chilling experience quickly taught us the folly of entering the river when an incoming tide carried with it the frigid waters from Hudson Bay. Consequently, our bathing schedule became directly dependent on the outgoing tide. The natural river current carried with it warmer waters from the inland area. During the month of June, every Sunday — morning, afternoon or evening, as the tides arranged — we managed our weekly swim. The swift current of the Hayes River limited our swimming to walking upstream and then allowing ourselves to be literally swept back to our private beach. The best I could manage when I attempted to swim against the current was to edge my way slowly towards the shore without being carried far downstream. However, the swift current of the water had a definite advantage. The mosquitoes preferred the stagnant waters of the muskeg.

Although we swimsuit-clad participants enjoyed the dip in the river, the children from the Indian village enjoyed it even more. A large audience always gathered on the shore to watch the weird antics of the school teacher and the store clerk.

The swimming season at York Factory ended with the school term. The school teacher left to spend his summer vacation amid Winnipeg's hustle and bustle. I realized that even buddy swimming in the Hayes River was somewhat foolhardy. While I looked forward to our Sunday dips, I did not risk continuing them alone.

My summer at York Factory was the two-hundred-fifty-seventh consecutive year that a ship sailed up the Hayes River to visit the trading post. Normally, a supply of trade goods was left in exchange for the winter's accumulation of fur. A few times, however, when the English held the fort, French vessels arrived and exchanged cannon balls for the winter's fur. The English, who did not wish to shatter their reputation for fair play, usually returned the following year and exchanged some of their cannon balls for whatever fur the French had managed to collect. For over a century, the exchange of cannon balls had remained nil, allowing York Factory to remain a Hudson's Bay Company post.

At the height of its glory, when ships from England brought supplies, York Factory served as the Canadian base for the Hudson's Bay Company. From the huge depot, York boats dispatched goods up the Hayes River through a series of small rivers and small lakes which eventually arrived at Norway House. From this location, the goods were freighted down Lake Winnipeg and into the heart of the continent. However, the route was now reversed. Goods traveled on trains from Winnipeg to Churchill and then were shipped to York Factory on schooners. Regardless of the port of origin, for centuries the natives had been on hand to await the arrival of the vessel.

On the morning of July first, I awoke to find the ever-fluctuating Indian population increased far beyond the non-surveyed boundaries of the village. Wigwams staked out campsite claims on the now abandoned playing field and any other island of solid ground large enough to accommodate the small abodes. Harold took one look at the population explosion and proclaimed: "The schooner will arrive tomorrow."

He was almost right as the schooner arrived late that evening.

Arrival of the ship meant festivity and festivity meant dancing. The natives built their own version of a community hall. This building was a community venture and in some fashion served every member of the community. The chief and his councillors met there, senior citizens found it to be an ideal spot to gather and to reminisce. Sometimes the younger children were permitted to use it as a playroom during inclement weather. When festive occasions arose, the building functioned marvellously as a dance hall. Three four-couple square dance sets had ample room to promenade left and kick up their heels without causing a traffic jam.

Harold had little interest in dancing. He much preferred to socialize with the district manager and sip a few cups of cheer with the officers from the ship. Not so his wife and his teenage daughters. They expressed their intention to attend the dance with or without a male escort. Consequently, a Bland-Robinson committee arrived at the unanimous decision that I should accompany the women.

Fortunately, a wooden walk extended for the full one and one half miles which separated the depot from the Indian village. This walk made it possible to arrive at the scene of the action without first soaking one's feet in the muskeg. I considered the dance at Gillam to be a real moccasin dance. A few moments at the York Factory ship-time dance proved sufficient for me to realize I was mistaken because here, only I wore shoes.

The dance was in progress when we arrived. I noticed that the natives had plenty of spring in their step, even without the benefit of snowshoes. When they "chased round the ladies," they did so by jumping at least two feet off the ground with each and every step. I attempted to use the gliding steps I associated with dancing, but I soon learned that the log floor permitted only the native dancing style. I changed to a reduced version of the jumping jive of the locals, but I still did a somewhat lifeless shuffle compared to them.

A native fiddler, accompanied by his squaw, provided live music. The musician rested the violin on his left ribcage just above his heart as he vigorously sawed away at a six-note melody. As if to avoid producing long and soothing notes, he choked his grip on the bow. This grip ensured no more than two thirds of the resin-coated horsehair ever swept over the strings. In order to ensure that the music had a steady beat, he tapped continuously with his heel. His accompanist peddled rapidly at an old organ and hammered out fistfuls of chords. What the duo lacked in musical tones, it more than compensated for in tempo. The fiddler's heel, the organist's down pedal and the dancers' feet all reached the lowest portion of their descent at the same time. The musicians were spelled off by a spring-powered gramophone and two double-sided records. This arrangement allowed us to dance to a grand total of five different melodies. In some mysterious way, the gramophone had found its way from the abandoned Port Nelson. The organ remained as a usable souvenir from York Factory's more populous days. But the origin of the violin, or how it became a portion of the native's few possessions, seemed to be shrouded in secrecy.

Although the night of revelry would have permitted me to slumber easily through high noon, high tide dictated the unloading schedule of the schooner. Harold woke me at the crack of dawn and cargo removal commenced with utter disregard for the condition of the unloading crew. Since my arrival at York Factory, I had lived in a world completely void of all time deadlines. This fact gave a double impact to the necessity of having to rise a good two and one half hours before my usual awakening time.

Such a radical deviation from the norm was, however, necessary. During the high water period, the twelve-foot tide allowed the schooner to be positioned at the end of the pier. While at low tide, the vessel had to be anchored near the centre of the river to avoid beaching. Consequently, cargo unloading took place when the tide permitted mooring the vessel in the most suitable unloading location.

Some of the natives boarded the vessel to move the cargo from the hold to the pier. Other natives took up positions on the pier to help lift the sacks and bales onto their fellow workers' backs. Once a native had 300 to 400 pounds on the business end of his packline, he would jog up the wooden walk to the warehouse and dump his load. To the natives, this practice was all fun and games. If unloading the schooner meant a race against the tide, packing the goods to the warehouse meant a race between the packers.

I was stationed in the warehouse to make a checklist of the unloaded goods. When I received the assignment it sounded simple, but I soon learned it involved more than reading the labels on the packages.

The only effort made to separate the goods at the pier end of the operation consisted of selecting bundles which made the most suitable arrangement for backpacking loads. This mix-and-match system resulted in one stockpile of flour, rice, sugar, salt, canned goods, baled goods and many other commodities hauled from the ship's hold, lying helter skelter on the warehouse floor. Invariably, the markings were well hidden. In order to read the labels I had to first separate and then repile the goods. Moreover, any help I might have obtained would have been of little use. The few local inhabitants who could read had found neither the time nor the opportunity to practise these skills after leaving school. While most natives could easily carry up to 500 pounds on their backs, few could either lift or carry much weight with their arms. Fortunately, the large floor area allowed me to separate one heap while the packers rushed to create another.

For several hours the carriers jogged up the walk, backpacking backbreaking loads, joking and laughing like a group of schoolboys embarking on their summer vacation. One trip for me carrying half their load would have caused every muscle in my body to tire to the point where I would not want to take a second trip. Still, as the day wore on, my lifting and sorting chores began to remind me that even muscles I had used frequently all my life could also tire. Long before the ebbing tide halted unloading operations, I vowed never again to wingding through the midnight hour when I knew ship unloading was the order of the following day. Spending a good eight hours, and possibly ten, in bed was a far more suitable way to spend the night. That evening showed many of the natives had made similar vows. I was among the few who attended the dance arranged as a conclusion for the ship unloading celebrations.

Approximately $15,000 worth of trade goods found their way from the ship's hold to the warehouse. At wholesale prices during the depression era, $15,000 purchased a lot of goods, but less than five per cent of the warehouse space was used to store them.

During the visit of the vessel, the word *Shamattawa* crept into a conversation between Harold and the Nelson River district manager. I am certain *Shamattawa* is a good Cree word with a definite meaning. However, the only meaning I ever managed to obtain suggested the word was the name of an outpost at the junction of the Echoing and God's rivers. For well over a century, York boats were used to freight goods between York Factory and *Shamattawa*. Since the rivers provided the only thoroughfare, no alternate method of transportation was ever implemented at that time.

Trade goods did not comprise the entire cargo carried by the schooner. Several crates were removed from the confines of the district manager's cabin. These crates contained the necessary components to assemble a radio transmitting and receiving set. Rather than risk the native packers breaking the crates and the valuable contents, I joined the ship's crew in carefully carrying them to the house. The short-wave radio training I received at the Winnipeg school could now be put to practical use. York Factory's name was added to the list of posts which enjoyed the most modern method of communication.

The district manager developed his interest in radio communication to the point where he was a ham enthusiast. He delayed the departure of the schooner long enough to ensure that the transmitter and the receiver were both properly assembled and in working order. We maintained ship-to-shore contact as the vessel sailed towards the river's mouth.

Although the unit was checked out and found to be in good working order, it obviously would not remain in that condition without having the batteries recharged. Therefore, erecting the windcharger assumed the top position on my job priority list.

Since he knew exactly where to look, Harold had no difficulty locating four fourteen-foot timbers. The timbers made ideal legs for a tower. A section of abandoned boardwalk furnished the necessary material to make cross braces and an upper platform. However, more than material was needed; we had to devise a method of erecting the structure which ensured it could withstand the force of the heavy winds. I suggested first setting the posts in the ground, similar to fence posts, and using them as a base on which to build. Harold, who prided himself on being a finished carpenter, desired first to construct the tower and then erect the finished product. We compromised and decided to sink the completed structure two feet into the swamp.

We marked off a square and I became a one-man excavating crew. After I reached a depth of approximately eighteen inches I hit frozen ground. I looked at the group of sidewalk superintendents who had gathered to watch and asked if any of them knew where I could find a pick. Jimmy McPherson, a Métis who was the closest neighbor to the staff house, suggested I leave the task until the next day.

When I first looked at my project the next morning, I began to doubt the wisdom of following Jimmy's advice. After half filling the hole, water from the surrounding muskeg had found its own level. Despite this apparent problem, I found myself able to dig the remaining eight inches without difficulty once this murky liquid was removed from the scene of operations.

I now had the necessary excavation, but I did not have an assembled tower to splash into it. With help from Harold, a form for assembling the structure was soon traced out on the spongy ground. Securing cross braces to the timbers came easy. Within an hour I had the completed assembly lying on the ground. The tower just needed to be muscle-powered into position.

During my digging and carpentry efforts, a large audience stood around or sat on the boardwalk and gave free advice. Nothing, not even the swarming throngs of mosquitoes, seemed to deter them, although occasionally cries of *kewatin, kewatin* (north wind, north wind) indicated they found the insects a bit annoying. However, as I hammered home the last spike in the last brace, I accidentally hit a hidden button which operated an automatic signal. Suddenly, they all found important business elsewhere and I was left to my own devices to change the tower from a horizontal to a perpendicular position.

By using the leverage I obtained as I lifted one of the ends, I easily placed the base at the edge of the hole. I then lifted the end designed to be the top of the tower. The structure followed the path of least resistance since it slid into the hole, until the base hit the side of the excavation. When the structure hit the side it stopped sliding. I stopped lifting and the structure dropped to the ground. Harold and one of his sons came to my rescue and we dragged on the tower until the base end no longer straddled the hole. While I lifted, the father-son team pulled, pried and shoved at the base. Suddenly, our efforts were rewarded with a gigantic splash. Without changing direction to avoid either people or things, the swamp water and mud rose and covered us. As I looked at the now-in-place tower that had displaced the muck, I was a happy mess.

After wiping the mud from his face, Harold produced a level. We assured ourselves that we had the tower wedged in a truly upright position. As I began to refill the hole, my audience reappeared.

Once erected, the wind charger functioned perfectly. It mattered little if the wind was *kewatin* or if it blew from some other direction. At York Factory, the air current was usually more than sufficient to send an ample charging current into the batteries.

Although all the equipment was in first-class working order, the radio dismally failed as a communication medium. Port Harrison on the eastern side of Hudson Bay was assigned as our control station. However, due to atmospheric conditions, the direction of the antennae or some other unexplainable phenomenon, I managed to hear Port Harrison only twice and I never received a reply to my C.Q.'s.

The York boats, which had been used to haul freight for generations, fell victim to the ravages of time. The last boat made its last trip to *Shamattawa* the previous year. Its remains rested on the river bottom near the outpost pier. The loss of the ship, though, did not spell the end of the system. The schooner brought the necessary material to allow a replacement to be built immediately.

Strategically located on the bank of a creek within easy access of high tide water, stood a boathouse. All the necessary tools, even a boiler for steam-bending the planks, remained in the building. In the past, Jimmy McPherson was employed as a boat builder. As if the layoff of several years had never occurred, Jimmy McPherson and three other Metis reopened the shipyard. As a result, I could have my turn at being sidewalk superintendent. Periodically, I visited the shipyard to watch the progress. If plans were used to build the ship, I never saw them. Despite this apparent shortcoming, every piece of wood was perfectly cut and trimmed to fit, the planks curved just the right amount and the ribs and keel fitted like a meticulously tailored garment.

Extended lunch breaks and flexible hours were a couple of the fringe benefits this low-salaried, non-union shipbuilding crew enjoyed. If a task higher on their list of priorities than shipbuilding required doing, they did it first. Around two thirty one afternoon, I dropped in to visit the boathouse. One of the erstwhile shipwrights, returning from lunch, followed me through the door. "Where have you been?" enquired one of his mates.

"Over bodying up to the widow," came the straightforward reply.

"Is she in a bodying up mood?" asked the questioner as he made no attempt to hide his interest.

"Sure is," replied the late arrival and his eyes shone brighter than the afternoon sun.

"Then I will go visit her for awhile myself," stated the interested inquirer. He laid down his tools and began walking rapidly in the direction of the Indian village.

This demonstration of the shipbuilders' unwavering loyalty to the company which paid their wages so impressed me that I decided any words from me calculated to encourage greater achievement were best kept to myself.

However, without any advice or prodding from either me or Harold the boat was completed, floated and found to be completely seaworthy.

Even though the radio had failed miserably as a message carrier, the moccasin telegraph functioned as effectively as it had for centuries. One evening as we seated ourselves at the supper table, Mrs. Bland informed us that the treaty payment party had left Gillam. Through experience Harold learned when his wife made such a statement there was no need to question her source of information. We spent the next day preparing the store for the rush of customers with spending money.

It took only twenty-four hours to justify Harold's faith in the sixth sense of the Indians. The drone of an outboard motor announced the arrival of visitors the next evening, as we closed the store for dinner. We warned the household and went to welcome our guests. We met an RCMP constable from Gillam, an RCMP inspector and a government doctor as they made their way along the wooden walkway from the pier. Normally, the constable wore suitable travelling garb such as denim trousers, an open collar shirt and a coat sweater, but today he wore his uniform. The inspector wore a sports jacket and grey flannel slacks. The doctor wore riding breeches, high-topped boots, a wide-brimmed hat and a windbreaker, but a mosquito net was the most noticeable item of the doctor's dress. This net dropped from the brim of his hat and covered his face, neck and shoulders. Obviously, it fell far short of providing the desired protection because a multitude of tiny lumps covered the portion of the fair skin which the netting was designed to protect. These lumps gave adequate proof that sandflies found his hide much to their liking.

By the time we returned to the staff house the Bland children had finished their evening meal. A clean tablecloth and place settings for the visitors, Harold and myself was set. Like the telecasters on a pregame warm-up show, Harold and the constable concentrated on exchanging their experiences from past treaty days. The rest of us gave eating our undivided attention and ignored the story-tellers.

If the arrival of a ship meant time to have a dance, then treaty day meant time to have a ball. Again, Harold's interests lay in spending the evening swapping yarns and having the odd drink with the visitors while the interests of Mrs. Bland and her older girls lay in swapping square dance partners at the wingding.

My earlier experiences taught me that dancing until the wee morning hours was not the ideal way to prepare for a busy day. I also knew that I was faced with the alternative of attending the dance or of listening to Harold and the constable attempting to top each other's stories; neither alternative offered any chance of rest until well past midnight. In some instances, decisions are easy to make and this was one of those instances. I escorted the ladies to the dance.

As the evening wore on, the crowd at the dance continued to grow. Obviously, word by moccasin telegraph travelled far and wide as natives I had never seen before arrived and appeared eager to join in the festivities. On the way home, I noticed newly erected teepees and tents overflowed the Indian village; several also were erected on the now-abandoned baseball field.

The following morning, as I followed Harold from the living quarters, the sight of twenty to thirty natives eagerly awaiting the opening of the store gave due warning that a day of hectic trading lay ahead. Although they all had visions of scalping the Hudson's Bay Company, these were friendly natives; also, they would be playing the scalping game with white man's rules. These odds left me with approximately the same risk of being taken for a loss as a professional gambler takes when he deals from a stacked deck. Even so in my starved-for-sleep condition, I could think of far more pleasant ways to pass the day than facing wave after wave of momentarily affluent Indians.

On the north wall of the store, a bench, large enough to seat eight people crowded together, reached from the door to the west counter. This bench provided an ideal seating arrangement for the older members of the tribe. It served as a marvelous vantage point from which to greet the transient members when they came to part with their recently acquired wealth. Greeting friends one had not seen since the last treaty day added additional excitement to the gala occasion.

In what seemed to be a wild desire to exchange their money for something of value before the Hudson's Bay Company realized that no use could be made of paper dollars, the Indians crowded, pushed and shoved like shoppers at a bargain basement sale. However, once they arrived at the counter, patience became the order of their day. While one customer exhausted his resources, his fellows stood back and made no attempt to interrupt.

Few, if any, of the natives were slaves to the tobacco habit. Food and other essentials normally held top priority on their shopping list. When funds permitted, a small package of cigarettes or a ten-cent package of tobacco might be their final purchase. Today, however, a tin of fifty cigarettes or a large can of tobacco invariably came first on their purchase list. In fact, their entire spending session took place with reckless abandon. The women had money to spend as they saw fit, and most of them saw fit to buy brightly colored prints.

At the start of the day Harold provided me with a small supply of silver. Since the natives considered those people who left the store with money in their pockets a little off base, a small supply proved to be sufficient. At the end of the spending spree, leftover money could be returned to the company coffers to be recirculated next year at treaty time. Frequently, the father asked for one or two dollars worth of change. He would then distribute equal amounts to each of his children. Invariably, the youngsters spent their allowance on *sweety-suck* (candies). Attempts to serve them quickly refreshed my memory of the difficulty I had deciding what to buy with my five cents when, as a boy, I accompanied my parents to town on Saturday night. None of the young Indians had been sufficiently indulged to know the different tastes of the goodies we offered, but they somehow managed to make their selections and leave the store with their parents. Although all members of the family were rendered penniless, they had at least made themselves happy.

Walter Gordon managed the post at *Shamattawa*. Officially, York Factory directed the smaller post's activities, but since my arrival at the big white house, no communication between the two posts had taken place. Consequently, one evening when two of the Bland children came running into the house to tell us of a canoe from *Shamattawa* approaching, both Harold and myself were taken by surprise.

We expected, of course, that Walter would be on hand when the schooner arrived with his trading supplies — what we did not know was when to expect the schooner. Walter had better mail service than we had. He told us the schooner expected to leave Churchill August first. Therefore, he decided to arrive a bit early. This early arrival permitted him to find accommodation for his wife and his family, to check on the progress of the York boat and to arrange for a crew to tow it up the river.

The already-floated York boat lay at anchor, waiting to begin service as a freight-towing barge. With several members of the *Shamattawa* Indian Band vacationing at York Factory since treaty time, the required crew was readily available. Only one of the cluster of cottages which originally occupied the post compound still remained. However, one of these cottages easily filled Walter's needs. The last resident vacated the premises and left a kitchen range and a dining room table. A couple of benches, augmented with the sleeping bags and cooking utensils his family later brought, furnished the dwelling to his satisfaction. By noon of the first day, Walter completed his pre-boat, pre-family chores and now all he had to do was wait.

He elected to spend most of his waiting time in my company. I found him to be an excellent instructor in guiding my efforts to learn the Cree language. He congratulated me on my progress, but he also advised that if I wished to become really fluent I should follow the example set by Harold and himself and try a blanket dictionary. Several of the Cree girls certainly had much more to offer than a comprehensive book course in the native language, but neither the company nor the natives condoned a common-law relationship. The laws of Canada made marriage to an Indian woman a nondissolvable union. The rules of the Hudson's Bay Company called for instant dismissal when such a union took place. As a result, I was far from ready to give up the freedoms of bachelorhood for the restrictions and the responsibilities that marriage imposed. Continuing to speak in broken Cree provided a much more desirable alternative to paying the costs that would have resulted from following Walter's suggestion.

On the afternoon of August first, I spent considerable time attempting to contact the schooner. Finally my efforts met with success as the M.S. *Fort Severn* was on her way. Although the radio gave definite confirmation that the ship left on the date Walter relayed, the population explosion in the native village was confirmation enough.

This schooner visit also created a slight rise in the white population. Walter's assistant, Norman, arrived in order to aid with the counting and sorting of the trade goods for *Shamattawa.*

Norman traced his ancestry back through at least three generations of Hudson's Bay Company servants. His parents were one of the trust account families who still lived in a small log cabin near the center of the white community. During his stay at York, Norman never wore the black denim trousers and colored shirts the rest of us found so serviceable. Every morning he arrived at the store wearing a freshly laundered white shirt and a pair of grey flannel slacks. The knife-edge crease in his slacks was invariably sharpened overnight. Since his mother relied on a scrubboard, water heated in a container placed on top of a woodburning oil drum stove, and a sad iron to do her washing chores, she must have labored long every evening over her son's laundry. I found myself wondering how Norman dressed at *Shamattawa* before leaving his bachelor quarters to work in the store.

The age-old custom of a dance preceding ship-unloading day formed an unbreakable precedent. The two previous dances had also fitted me into an unbreakable precedent as I provided Hudson's Bay Company representation at the social functions.

The tides from the bay set a more lenient schedule for cargo unloading than the previous trip. The tides did not peak until twelve o'clock which postponed the starting time from five o'clock until ten o'clock in the morning. Everyone had the opportunity to obtain some much-needed rest before beginning the strenuous unloading task. Due to the influence of the Depression, supplies were seldom, if ever, back ordered. Never-the-less, some items for York Factory still did not arrive with the schooner's first visit. Since the responsibility for sorting, piling and counting the majority of the stock fell to Walter and Norman, my assigned duties were minimal. All signs pointed to an easy day.

Norman took a position on the dock to direct the packers to a separate warehouse for the *Shamattawa* stock or to the main warehouse for the York Factory stock, depending on the goods they carried. Walter took a position in the separate warehouse.

The packers, however, did not follow our prearranged plan. They based their total effort on gathering a load, racing with it to a warehouse and letting it drop. To them, only speed mattered. Sorting and piling neatly were trivials that those of us able to read and write could look after. Norman found himself at a loss to persuade his fellow Metis to follow his orders. Since ample space existed in the main warehouse, we changed plans and had all loads dumped there. Walter and I sorted and piled as the packers dropped their loads. Even though we worked steadily, several heaps still remained unseparated after the schooner left.

Before the M.S. *Fort Severn* disappeared from view, loading of the York boat commenced. The natives selected for the crew did the necessary packing and stowing of cargo. They abandoned their customary practice of dropping the sacks and bales in haphazard heaps. With great care they placed every item in the position best suited to provide an equal distribution of weight. This placement ensured that the vessel would ride with an even keel and place less drag on the towlines as they pulled it through the water. Until the incoming tide signalled departure time, the loaded boat rode at anchor.

Eight men comprised the crew. Four men rode the boat and with the use of long poles, they made certain she remained in open water. Four men were harnessed to the vessel with long towropes as they walked along the shore. Every half hour the walkers and the polers changed place. During the first lap of the journey, the strength of the incoming tide forced the men on the shore to jog at a brisk clip in order to keep the towline taut.

After watching the departure of the scow we returned to survey the mess of goods scattered over the floor of the separate warehouse. Timbers eight to ten inches thick were used in the construction of this building. For some reason, the windows were fitted with iron bars. Heavy plank doors fitted with enormous locks provided the only access. We decided to leave the York Factory merchandise that had been carried to this warehouse right where it lay. Security presented no problem and the dwindling store stock could be replenished from this location as easily as it could be from any other part of the compound.

Walter and Norman did not accompany the York boat. Their canoes were powered with outboard motors which could travel at least three times faster. Since a second trip of the scow would be required to transport the balance of the *Shamattawa* stock, Walter wanted to be on hand to supervise the loading. Norman also had a reason; he wanted to spend his birthday at home.

Other than the general community knowledge of it being past thirty and below forty, I have no idea which anniversary the *Shamattawa* assistant was about to celebrate. In any event, his father approached the father of a fifteen-year-old girl to arrange a marriage for his son on the eve of the celebration. Even though Norman was considered the most eligible bachelor in the Metis community, the difference in ages caused the concerned father to refuse. As he left to check the unloading of the scow cargo at *Shamattawa*, neither Norman's manner nor his expression showed the slightest trace of disappointment. Also, no difference was noted in either the girl's expression or her behavior as she continued to enjoy the freedom and the games of childhood.

The few weeks sandwiched between the departure of the supply ship and the grubstaking of the trappers formed the slack season of the year. Harold took advantage of this slack period to promote me to *kitchie ogamo* (big boss) because he wished to leave for a vacation in Winnipeg. Excursions to the metropolis formed the highlight of his life; for him, the ultimate luxuries were living in a hotel, riding in taxis and availing himself of ample supplies of alcoholic beverages. The holiday party consisted of Bland and his two oldest girls while the rest of the family remained at York Factory.

Harold's decision to leave the larger portion of his family behind proved to be a definite benefit to me. During normal trading, my limited knowledge of Cree created little difficulty. However, with the departure of Bland and the swift, sure announcement through the moccasin telegraph, all natives knew that a young, green trader was in charge of York Factory. The activity at the post could no longer be classed as slow or even as normal. Natives who were total strangers to me suddenly arrived and they all had one purpose in mind. They wanted to increase their unpaid credit balance to the highest possible level. By looking through the post's extensive credit records, I easily established that most of these visitors already owed more than half of what a good season's fur catch would cover. The written word provided ample proof that no further grubstakes should be forthcoming. However, natives who had little difficulty in eloquently expressing their need for credit and strongly asserting how they could promptly repay, suddenly found themselves unable to understand a word I said, regardless of my use of language when I informed them "No more debt."

The two oldest Bland boys, who spent their time in the store, during their father's absence, came to my rescue. Acting as my interpreter provided the boys with a virtually unlimited supply of fun and games. My limited knowledge of Cree enabled me to readily understand that my refusals for credit were being presented with far more descriptive adjectives and phrases than I had voiced in English. Phrases such as, "I would be foolish to advance further credit," were translated into phrases like, *"Ocamassis is no atugeye."*

While the quoted translations were far from verbatim, the natives received the main point of the message. Many of them left the store mumbling intended barbs such as, "It is too bad the clerk does not have a slight amount of authority so he could give me a slight amount of debt."

Before Harold's departure, arrangements were made to cut the winter's supply of firewood. The Anglican mission owned a gasoline engine and a circular saw. Providing two conditions were met, Archdeacon Faries did not hesitate to allow the Hudson's Bay Company to use this equipment. The two conditions were that we had to pay the native crew he selected to operate the equipment and we had to furnish our own gasoline.

A small shed which was designated as an oil house contained several drums of gasoline and other petroleum products. Potential customers who browsed through the store prevented me from leaving the premises unattended. I elected to add the duties of oil house supervisor to the responsibilities of the woodcutting engineer. His book learning was not sufficient to enable him to read written English, but experience had taught him how to use his sense of smell to select gasoline, kerosene and other products. Unfortunately, this sense of smell was not sufficiently attuned to distinguish between high-octane and ordinary gas. This deficiency resulted in ten gallons of airplane fuel being taken for use in the sawing operation. The fuel was stored for the self-named "flying priest," Father Paul Schulte. Father Schulte had visited native communities along the coast of Hudson Bay for several years, but for some reason he ignored the inland communities.

Possibly due to the more powerful fuel, a leaking head gasket caused the saw engine to stall shortly after the woodcutting operation began. The native engineer again demonstrated that his inability to read presented no great handicap. He had no need to check a list of dealers or study the instructions for replacing head gaskets. Within half a day, the Indian made a return trip to Port Nelson where he obtained a new head gasket from the abandoned stock in the deserted construction site. The gasket provided a leak-proof seal between the cylinder block and the engine head. As a result, the repaired engine functioned perfectly, even with the high-octane gas. Soon the neatly piled, raft-length logs quickly became a heap of firewood sticks.

About three weeks after Harold returned he discovered that the gasoline was taken from the wrong drum. I then received the necessary advice about which fuel was to be used for woodcutting and outboard motors and which fuel was stored for the flying priest. The ten gallons were later replaced from a barrel of regular gasoline. The native provided a suitable target on which Harold could vent his feelings, but I doubt if the Indian ever learned about the mistake. No special markings designated the airplane fuel as distinct from the post's stock and the drum was situated nearest to the door. If I had made the trip to the oil house, I would doubtlessly have tapped the same drum.

Six months later, word came to dump all gas stored at Hudson's Bay posts for use by Father Schulte, because his name was placed on the list of suspected German spies. The numerous photographs the flying priest took of natives provided ample foundation for this suspicion. As a group of Indians or Eskimos stood on the shores of Hudson Bay, he took snap shots from every possible angle. These photographs recorded a detailed, pictorial map of every possible landing spot along the entire coast. Unless a study of Reverend Schulte's pictures established that landing a task force on the bleak, undeveloped shores of Hudson Bay would end in total disaster, no other evidence exists to indicate that the strategists for the German war machine ever used the data he collected.

For the balance of my stay at York Factory, the comradeship which developed between the Bland boys and myself during their father's absence continued. Throughout the duck-hunting season this friendship enabled me to establish my prowess as a hunter. Every Saturday one of the boys and sometimes both, together with a couple of their friends, would accompany me on a fowl-hunting safari. I soon learned that York Factory methods differed greatly from those used on the prairies. During the period of low tide we would launch a canoe and take advantage of the river current to journey to a midstream island about one half mile towards the Hudson Bay. Once we arrived at our destination we selected one of the numerous blinds that dotted the island and made ourselves as comfortable as the damp ground permitted. Like most of the man-made buildings in the area, these structures were old. They probably were erected during a generation when people relied on bows and arrows for weapons.

From our hidden position we waited until the incoming tide, or some other factor, caused the birds to seek the calm and sheltered waters of the island. At first, I shot at everything I considered to be within shotgun range, but my youthful guides soon taught me the errors of my ways. Not only were they fluent in Cree and in English, they also were proficient in duck quacking and in goose honking. The boys would call both species of fowl until they swooped in to land about ten yards from the blind. Even though I tried to condition myself not to shoot until I saw the whites of their eyes, seldom did they get that close. The excitement of one or the other of my companions would cause him to yell, "Shoot *ocamassis*, shoot!"

We primarily took these outings to provide food for the dining room table; any sport involved was merely a fringe benefit. Consequently, shooting fowl that had been lured into impossible-to-miss range fulfilled our purpose. Moreover, this strategy did not leave a multitude of slightly wounded or frightened birds which could warn their fellows not to frequent the island. Unfortunately, since the peak of the incoming tide controlled both occurrences, the time to vacate the island coincided with the arrival of the largest flocks of incoming birds. The alternative to leaving meant waiting on the island until the next tide change. Although the duck blinds, built on soggy ground, provided excellent concealment, they dismally failed to provide comfort. Both waiting and paddling against the current imposed endurance tests which neither my companions nor myself had any desire to take. Invariably, we abandoned the hunt.

Initially on the return journeys, in case a flock of birds passed within range, I left a loaded shotgun in the canoe. It never occurred to me that retrieving any kill would have been impossible due to the powerful current. On one trip, a dozen or so ducks passed within 150 feet in front of the canoe. One of my companions grabbed the gun and blasted, but he missed the ducks and, fortunately, my head as well. From then on, I made certain that the gun carried in the canoe was not loaded and all the shells were in my parka pocket. The breeze of shotgun pellets passing near one's ear teaches a lesson which far surpasses any obtained through the conventional book learning method.

Like the balance of Manitoba, York Factory enjoys four distinct seasons and like most seasons, their duration varies from year to year. The beginning and end dates shown on a calendar are seldom accurate. A short autumn marked my year at York Factory. One day we enjoyed an Indian summer, but the next morning snow covered the ground and a layer of ice formed at the river's edge. Within a week, a trip for water meant walking on ice and using an ice chisel. It also became necessary to keep a log of the tide changes. Visual inspection could no longer determine the direction of water flow. However, because the ice itself was salt free, it could be used to fill the water barrel whenever the need outweighed the chiselling effort.

While the covering of ice meant more work for the water carrier, it also meant fishing without standing around and waiting for a bite. Several of the local residents, including the two Bland boys, walked approximately to midstream, cut a hole in the ice and dropped a weighted line which secured several baited hooks. Since the depth of the hooks varied from ten feet to two feet, no concern existed about fish striking a deep or a shallow bait. Although every trip to the lines did not mean enough fish for supper, the catch was certainly sufficient to warrant the effort. It took a good catch to provide enough fish to feed seven hungry youngsters and three adults.

Two and a half centuries of human settlement had persuaded the fur-bearing animals to retreat from the dangers that accompanied close proximity to the post. However, ptarmigan had little fear of human settlement. Occasionally a flock would land on the patch of frozen muskeg that constituted someone's backyard. By stalking, a person could easily manage to arrive within stick-throwing distance of these birds. Unfortunately, my stick-throwing abilities fell far short of the skills required to make such a weapon a deadly missile. Since the ptarmigan had no intention of prolonging their migrations in order to allow me the necessary time to learn new skills, I used the modern and improved hunting method — a twenty-two-caliber rifle. Frequently, as many as three shots could be fired before the birds became sufficiently alarmed to take flight. Then, even though they retreated from the danger zone, they considered a distance of fifty to 100 yards to be sufficient for the first retreat. Once they landed, the steps of stalking, firing and retreating could be repeated; frequently, a third stalking and firing could be accomplished. On the third retreat, the birds invariably flew well beyond the hunter's field of vision. Since the size of a ptarmigan is only slightly greater than the size of a well-fed pigeon, it took a successful hunt to produce enough of these game birds to form a meat course for a meal in the Bland household.

The buildings, the dress of the natives and the general way of life gave the impression that time stood still at York Factory, but the aging process continued. Special days, such as New Year's, birthdays and Christmas occurred with the same regularity with which they occurred in the rest of the world. Christmas at York, however, differed from those I had previously experienced. It lacked the overabundance of commercialism common in the more advanced portions of the globe. Even so, a marked increase in the store activity became noticeable around the middle of December. Only when they had sufficient justification did the native trappers return from their trapping grounds; the religious Christmas celebrations provided sufficient justification. Once they arrived at the post, trading became their number-one priority. Normally, a credit balance, the size of which directly depended on the success of the person's trapline, remained on the books after the person left the store. During the next few days, the women of the trapper's family did their utmost to remove this balance from the company books.

Serving these customers could be accomplished without uttering a word. One pound of tea and two pounds of sugar were the first items on their lists. If a substantial balance existed, canned milk was added. We carried two grades of tea and automatically I would hand the customer the cheaper grade. Occasionally, my service would meet with a head swivel, a finger pointed at the better grade and the words, "oma maggon" (that one).

The tea parties moved from cabin to cabin. Sometimes a hostess would make two trips to the store for supplies in one afternoon. When this happened we knew that the success of her party had caused it to last longer than normal.

Not only had the ways of the whiteman taught the natives about drinking tea, it had also taught them about drinking beverages made from fermented fruits and grains. With raisins, cornmeal, yeast cakes and brown sugar, some of the more venturesome concocted a form of corn liquor. On a couple of occasions I found myself faced with two choices. I could sample the product or offend a group of drunken Indians. Rather than offend our customers I joined Harold in the coward's way out and sampled the product. The liquor had a definite effect on me. While the second gulp was passing my tonsils, the first gulp was making me sick to my stomach. Liquid on the way up meeting liquid on the way down creates a situation that the human digestive tract was never designed to accept. The system permits everything to travel only one way. Whenever I sipped York Factory brew, that way immediately became up. I doubt if any of the alcohol ever remained in my system long enough to enter my blood stream.

Although neither Harold nor myself approved of this home-brewing practice, there was little we could do to stop it. The laws of the land prohibited all treaty Indians from the partaking of intoxicating beverages, but it would have been ludicrous to summon the RCMP from Gillam to come and lay charges. Travel by either dogteam or canoe, depending on the season, meant at least a couple of weeks would elapse before the message arrived at Gillam and the constable arrived at York. When the officer arrived from Gillam, he would have to find the alleged offender, locate a witness for the Crown and some trace of the evidence.

If an Indian decided to hide in the dwarf forest, a white man could search forever without finding him. If by some remote chance, a witness for the Crown could be found on the reserve, the balance of the tribe would be available to serve as witnesses for the accused. In any case, all evidence would have been consumed ten days to a fortnight previously because the hungry dogs loved the leftover mash. Nor could we refuse to sell anyone any of the necessary ingredients as all were items purchased regularly for legitimate purposes.

Lack of whiteman's justice did not free the natives from disciplinary action, however. On one occasion word drifted down from the village that a group of revelers had gotten out of hand. Quickly following this rumor came word that the chief and his counselors had decided on and enforced the necessary disciplinary action. It worked and there was no repeated trouble.

Santa Claus visited the Indian children whenever the proceeds from their father's trapline permitted. Seldom, if ever, did he bring toys. He concentrated on a greater need and filled a few fortunate stockings with raisin bannock and other goodies, giving the Indian children the shock of a lifetime by filling their stomachs until they stretched.

Due to the Christmas business we had sufficient raw fur on hand to warrant making a good-sized shipment. Harold estimated the shipment would make four bales; his years of experience enabled him to make a well-educated guess. When the pressing operation was completed, four bales stood ready for shipment to Hudson's Bay house in Winnipeg.

The first step was a dog team trip to Gillam. Although I realized that the snowshoes would produce blisters on my feet, I readily agreed to accompany Jim on the trip. After much begging from Mrs. Bland, one of the Bland boys, and myself, Harold reluctantly agreed to let the boy go along on the trip.

Jim let it be known in no uncertain terms that he would have preferred taking his own son rather than travel with either, or for that matter, both of us. Since he had a choice of taking the job on our terms or not at all, he agreed to our terms.

With snowshoes, the young boy walked over the soft snow with greater ease than I could walk on clear pavement without them. Although he held up his end at breaking trail, when we made camp that first night Jim started to grumble about having to do so many of the camp chores by himself, such as feeding the dogs. I reminded him that if he did not want to be teamster there were several others at York who did. The grumbling stopped as quickly as it started. There is little doubt that John could have provided greater assistance, with his years of tripping experience. In addition, although the boy and myself did the cooking, built the windshelter and looked after the campfire, our presence necessitated additional cooking, shelter-building and camp-fire fuel. Far fewer comforts would have been sufficient for Jim and his son.

On the second day an impassable stretch of rapids forced us to detour from the smooth bed of river ice on the toboggan trail. As if nature had contrived to block our progress, we reached a bank that was too steep for a team of semi-starved dogs to manage while pulling a loaded toboggan. Even when Jim and I provided extra lugging the dogs found it impossible to haul the loaded conveyance up the hill.

We had to remove the four bales of fur. Carrying a bale from the storage room to the toboggan had been an easy lift for Jim and myself, but I soon learned that carrying a bale of fur along a floored corridor differed greatly from carrying one up a steep bank that provided treacherous footing at best. It took the combined efforts of Jim and myself to roll the bales like giant snowballs up the hill, one at a time. Whenever the need for an extra push arose, we found it necessary to pause first in order to restore our energies.

This first exercise in winter portaging proved merely to be a warm-up exercise. The river wandered everywhere, finding the path of least resistance while the rail line from Gillam to Port Nelson followed a direct route. To avoid travelling extra miles, we followed the well-established practice of leaving the river to follow the rail line. Since the line had been abandoned before any bridges were built, every creek we crossed meant we had to unload the toboggan and manhandle the bales down one bank and up the other.

For me, the rail line had an advantage that far outweighed the inconvenience of unloading and reloading. Most of the snow had blown away from the abandoned rail bed over which we travelled, but sufficient snow remained to allow the toboggan to slide while I walked without snowshoes. However, my companions continued to wear their snowshoes and they strode along with a spring in every step.

The night turned extremely cold. To compensate for the low temperature we built a fire larger than usual. Although we slept with our feet toward the blaze the young lad complained of having cold feet. I placed my parka over the bottom of his sleeping bag. During the night the garment was inadvertently kicked into the fire. The next morning I salvaged my wolverine-fringed parka hood from the edge of the fire pit. Fortunately we had a Hudson Bay blanket along for extra warmth and I travelled with it wrapped around me for the balance of the journey. This substitute parka served its purpose remarkably well because it provided more actual warmth than my parka. However, the extra weight and restricted arm movement that resulted from wearing a blanket eliminated any thought I might have had about not replacing my burned garment.

As we neared Kettle Rapids a rifle-toting guard came to greet us. A wartime security measure decreed that the isolated bridge be patrolled twenty-four hours a day. During the winter the train made one monthly return trip over the bridge. Patrolling one hundred yards of track for a full working shift was an occupation that would make even a hermit feel lonely. Consequently, the few travelers who passed that way were greeted rather than challenged and even my unusual garb failed to elicit so much as a question.

Concealed under the bridge was a cabin which housed the security guards and provided a few primitive comforts. We spent a lunch break with the two off-duty sentries. When we left, the patrolman mounting guard escorted us to the western edge of his beat and pressed us for our promise to drop in again on the return trip.

When we reached the outskirts of Gillam, pride in my appearance took precedence over my need for comfort. I anticipated Jim's next move and I laid the blanket on top of the toboggan. He followed his usual practice and allowed the dog team a brief rest before urging them to a full gallop for the last lap of the journey. My heavy woolen sweater, big gauntlet mitts and winter cap with its fur-lined ear flaps provided sufficient protection from the cold during this brief sprint to the company store.

The Gillam post manager measured off a couple of yards of duck and directed me to a one-roomed cabin. The cabin was the residence and workshop of Maryanne, the official village parka-maker. Since she owned the only sewing machine in the Indian community she had a monopoly on a good portion of the custom tailoring business. While her four preschool children watched with great interest (I was a cash customer so they would eat for another day), she stretched a length of white thread around my chest and knotted it to indicate the size of garment required. I held out my arm so she could measure the sleeve length but she shook her head; apparently she considered any further measurements to be absolutely unnecessary. I left her the duck and the hood from my previous garment and arranged to pick up the completed garment the following day.

She charged me a flat fee of one dollar and a half for the tailoring. For that fee I didn't expect perfection; when I tried on the garment, I realized I did not get any more than I expected. The long gauntlets of my mitts compensated for the short sleeves and the tail of my black woolen sweater hung three inches below my newly acquired garment.

In March 1940 a posting to Churchill affected me personally, as if I was placed in a time machine. Suddenly I found myself ejected from the peace and tranquility of a past era into the hustle and bustle of the present. My journey to Gillam gave me my last taste of the century-old customs of York Factory. I left as I arrived. My baggage rode on a toboggan while I trudged along as the unnecessary member of the dog team crew.

Churchill

Cash Register Trading Post is a term which aptly describes the Bay operations at Churchill. By Depression day standards the settlement was booming. In the summer when the docks were open, the male population numbered approximately one hundred and thirty; all of them were employed. There were also approximately fifteen white women who had permanent homes in the townsite. As a result of this combination, the bulk of the store business differed greatly from that of a fur trading post.

Toiletry items were not carried at York Factory but were in great demand at Churchill. In fact, the majority of the merchandise carried could also be found in the general stores that serviced the small communities in the southern part of the province. Although Indian beads and other goods did make up part of the stock, fur buying and native trade occupied only a fraction of the total time spent doing business. Despite this, fur trading was profitable and more than held its own with the general store business.

Manager Bob Urquhart had risen to a district accountant from an apprentice clerk in a period of fifteen years. As a district accountant he had been stationed at Hudson's Bay house in Winnipeg. When the need for an experienced manager at Churchill occurred, his love for the north induced him to arrange a transfer. Over the past couple of years an increasing number of Bay customers in the Churchill area decided to take their business to the opposition trader. Bob proved to be an excellent choice to remedy this situation and in six months he not only halted the trend but reversed it.

A couple of local winos told me about the good old days before Urquhart took over. Apparently, the Hudson's Bay Company store had housed some bang-up parties at that time. When the alcohol-spiked wine ran out they broke open a case of vanilla extract. Bob did not concentrate on building up the extract business, although a stock, sufficient to supply the baking needs of the community for a good ten years, stood neatly stacked in the far corner of the warehouse.

Bob also succeeded in building up the overall business of the store. Every train brought increasing orders of fresh meat and the in-season vegetables during the summer months. Although there was only one shipment per month in the winter and one per week in the summer, the entire supply of uncanned, unpickled and unpreserved foods was usually sold within three hours of the train's arrival. Before reaching the depot, the train frequently added a couple of hours to the time shown on the official schedule. However, it invariably arrived on the scheduled Sunday and each approximate noontime arrival warranted a Sunday afternoon opening of the Bay store. These extra hours became our busiest period of the week, due at least partly to the fresh food now available.

In less than a year after he had taken over the Churchill post, Bob created a need for additional storage space. Soon after my arrival, an icehouse, built to preserve perishable food during the summer, received its final coat of paint. Plans were already submitted for a separate warehouse that would ensure a sufficient supply of non-perishable merchandise would be on hand during the monthly winter delivery season.

The majority of Indians in the Churchill area were Chipewyan. The drastic difference in their facial features made it easy to distinguish them from the Cree. The Chipewyan eyes were smaller and their foreheads appeared to be lower. The Churchill natives also had two other distinguishing features; they grew taller and showed no evidence of having freely intermingled with the white race. I mastered very little of the Chipewyan tongue. The little I did master seemed to indicate that the language consisted of few words; each word was given several different meanings by pronouncing it in slightly different ways. Fortunately, lacking the ability to converse fluently with these people created little, if any, difficulty. There were similarities between the two Native tribes. Like the Cree women, a Chipewyan squaw knew exactly what she would buy before she left to go shopping.

At least half of the white matrons who dealt with the Hudson's Bay Company used a shopping method in direct contrast to that of the natives. I am certain that the majority of their shopping trips were initiated by an overwhelming urge to get out of their kitchens and that some ingredient required for a stewpot merely provided the justification. Shopping constituted a daytime outing. After browsing for an hour, white women might make some small purchase, or add a package of cigarettes to their husband's bill in order to prove to their own satisfaction the necessity of taking a break from their household chores. One woman spent her time checking the entire stock of groceries, cosmetics and housekeeping needs, seldom making a purchase. She justified her time by asking for items she had already ascertained we did not have in stock. Since cigarettes had a gross profit of one cent per pack and constituted a loss item, we made a greater profit from her nil purchase than we made from the cigarette purchasers.

When the snow began to melt Bob proudly announced that the post equipment included a half-ton, model A Ford truck. By sending the required fees to the motor vehicle branch in The Pas, he obtained driver's licenses for us and plates for the vehicle. The delivery service provided by the truck added to the company business. Once the need to carry their purchases home was eliminated the shoppers placed larger orders. A customer whose order warranted delivery was automatically assured of a ride home with the delivery run. Thus the truck offered an additional benefit to the relief-from-boredom excursions of the village matrons. One woman, old enough to be my mother, made a practice of arriving half an hour before the afternoon delivery. Bob, whose age group placed him in her generation, decided to relieve me of my chauffeuring chores for one trip. He did. The woman in question had her groceries brought in by train from The Pas for the next three weeks. Then, possibly because our prices were lower, she returned to the Bay.

To accommodate the white trade, Bob stocked the icehouse with various types of sausages, weiners and other prepared meats. One evening, two ladies with reputations indicating that good morals were not their prime concern, requested to make some selections from the ice house stock. As they were making their choices I noticed one of them slipped a garlic sausage down the front of her blouse. As we left with their selected items, I suggested that the secluded item should also be counted and paid for. "Oh," she said, "I'd forgotten about that." She calmly placed it back in the ice-packed container.

Soon after my arrival at Churchill, a native woman came into the store. She had no difficulty explaining her wants, but had great difficulty explaining how payment would be forthcoming. She kept pointing to the counter books and I kept reading names from them. Bob heard the commotion from his office in the corner of the store and immediately came to my rescue. The woman was a native Eskimo married to a former Hudson's Bay Company clerk. The ex-clerk enlisted in Canada's armed forces and was subsequently posted overseas. His pay assignment went directly to the Hudson's Bay Company and a weekly allotment was set aside to ensure that adequate funds provided for his wife and family.

I learned later the Eskimo name for Indians. Literally it translated into the enemy. I also learned that Eskimos are friendly people. This particular woman lived in the Indian village and, although her husband had been overseas for at least eighteen months, she was noticeably

Bill Robinson, author, sitting on cannon in front of York Factory.

York Factory (1922) during its boom years.
PUBLIC ARCHIVES CANADA

The author taking a brief rest while out ptarmigan hunting.

The Indians called the Hudson's Bay Company building at York Factory *Kitchie Waskahagan* (big white house). PHOTO BY A.B. McIVOR — HUDSON'S BAY CO.

Children saw wood in front of the Cree church in York Factory.

York Factory cemetery and remains of powder magazine.
PHOTO BY A.B. McIVOR — HUDSON'S BAY CO.

The old cannon in front of the York Factory warehouse.

Archdeacon and Mrs. Faries. On Sundays, two services were conducted
— one in the English church and another in the Cree church.

The seven children of Harold Bland, manager of the store at York Factory.

Natives outside cabin. PHOTO BY A.B. McIVOR — HUDSON'S BAY CO.

Native displays
a sturgeon in the inner
courtyard of York
Factory's store-
warehouse complex. →

**Indian squayshish (girls)
outside the store
warehouse at York
Factory.**
PHOTO BY A.B. McIVOR —
HUDSON'S BAY CO.

Interior of store at York Factory.   PHOTO BY A.B. McIVOR — HUDSON'S BAY CO.

Anglican church in Churchill.

Remains of old Fort Churchill — gun base at river mouth.

←**Trappers arrive at Churchill with a load of furs.**
PHOTO BY RICHARD
HARRINGTON
— HUDSON'S BAY CO.

Old cannon in front of the Hudson's Bay Company store at Churchill.

The *Fort Severn* anchored.
This schooner hauled freight from Churchill to York Factory. ➡

Terminal
elevator
at Churchill.

Hudson's Bay railway terminal at Churchill, c. 1928.
PUBLIC ARCHIVES CANADA

One of the relics from Churchill's construction days.

Interior of Hudson's Bay Company store at Churchill.

Hudson's Bay Company store with terminal elevators in the background.
HUDSON'S BAY CO.

Interior of Churchill store. The Indians liked the brightly colored cotton prints shown in the foreground.

Shacks and houses in the Indian village.

Wigwams at edge of the Indian village.
PHOTO BY DR. W. YOUKER —
HUDSON'S BAY CO.

One of the many settlements along the Churchill Railway.

Eastern arctic Eskimo *komatik* (sled) drawn by dogs and utilizing a fan hitch.
PHOTO BY N. ROSS — HUDSON'S BAY CO.

Albert's Boy and Curly.

Winter travel, Eskimo fashion.

Stones piled as guidepost markers at an Eskimo cemetery in the Repulse Bay area. PHOTO BY F. BRUMMER — HUDSON'S BAY CO.

White fox pelts hung out on a line to free the fur of sawdust. The sawdust was used as a final fur-cleaning agent, after the fat had been scraped from the inside of the hides.

Repulse Bay seen from the M.S. *Fort Severn.* This ship docked here only once a year — bringing the residents supplies and replies to letters written the previous year.

A welcome sight for the people of Repulse Bay — the break-up of ice. The ice mass would then sit offshore until a favorable wind and incoming tide brought it to shore again, where it would remain throughout the winter.

Native children playing near the water's edge.

Ready to depart from overnight camp constructed on the trail.
PHOTO BY WILLIAM GIBSON — HUDSON'S BAY CO.

Left to right: young harp seal, silver jar seal, square flipper seal. PHOTO BY J.G. CORMACK — HUDSON'S BAY CO.

An Eskimo ices the runners of his *komutik* by squirting water over them from his mouth. PHOTO BY N. ROSS — HUDSON'S BAY CO.

Eskimo in the process of icing *komutik* runners. One runner is already completed and starting to freeze — see the hoar frost starting to form. The other is still soft and is being patted smooth.

PHOTO BY W.F. JOSS — HUDSON'S BAY CO.

Dogs holding polar bear at bay.
PHOTO BY L.A. LEARMONTH — HUDSON'S BAY CO.

Taken at midnight while camping on return journey from Wager Inlet.

Dwelling house and oil shed at Repulse Bay. Every precaution was taken to preserve these frame buildings at the trading posts, as arctic lumber was more valuable than ivory. One such precaution consisted of an outside paint job every second year. HUDSON'S BAY CO.

Walrus.

**Establishing Wager Inlet post
c. 1926.** PUBLIC ARCHIVES CANADA

**Eskimo hauls up seal after
spearing it at a breathing hole.**
PHOTO BY P. PITSEOLAK —
HUDSON'S BAY CO.

R.M.S. *Nascopie* held in the ice at Repulse Bay.

**Stalking a seal with
the aid of a screen.**
PHOTO BY J. CORMACK —
HUDSON'S BAY CO.

**Hauling a ring seal
into the boat.**
PHOTO BY R.N. HOURDE —
HUDSON'S BAY CO.

pregnant.

Before the blessed event took place, her husband wrote her a "Dear Jane" letter. While spending a furlough in his homeland he had met a Scottish lass and now wished for his freedom in order to marry his new-found love, even though Canadian law forbid it. The Eskimo woman went to pieces. Apparently, even though he was not the only man in her life, he was the most important. Bob proved himself to be an able politician. As he read the letter out loud to her he did all he possibly could to soften the blow. Although I am certain his sympathies lay with the young soldier, his manner remained absolutely neutral. A few months later an official telegram arrived announcing the boy had been killed in action. His love triangle failed to have a happy ending.

During the summer months, the weekly train necessitated some track maintenance. One Sunday three section hands from Avery arrived to spend a night on the town. The beer parlour was closed and the local bootlegger soon depleted their funds.

Remembering the good old days before Urquhart took over, they arrived at the Hudson's Bay Company store. They requested a little credit to purchase a dozen bottles of vanilla but I felt extremely reluctant to open accounts for three men who might never again visit Churchill. From the suite above the store Bob overheard the heated discussion. He came down the stairs and explained clearly that he was not hesitant about turning away their type of business. They left in a huff and, to the best of my knowledge, never returned.

Around the first of August, a long-time manager from one of the Eskimo posts arrived in Churchill. He had just spent several months in Britain and spoke rather sparingly on most topics. But he spoke frequently about his wife. After their marriage she refused to leave Scotland, so every third year he would spend his furlough visiting her. The restricted conditions that the war placed on ocean travel made it mandatory to accept passage whenever it became available. Consequently, he found himself compelled to lay over for three weeks while waiting for the *Nascopie* to sail from Churchill on its northern trip. He enjoyed the solitary life an isolated post offered and found the village of Churchill too congested for his liking. Still, he considered it a superior waiting station compared to the larger centers such as Montreal or Winnipeg.

This semi-recluse spent very little of his time in the Hudson's Bay Company store. But when a party of natives arrived from Eskimo Point, he appeared as if by magic. Since the natives spoke little English and Bob spoke no Inuit, his volunteer services as an interpreter were much in demand. As the trappers placed several of their skins to one side, Bob looked questioningly at the volunteer interpreter. The natives' reasoning was quickly relayed. These furs were for the opposition retailer. In order to ensure that the Hudson's Bay Company paid a good price for their furs the rival trader had to stay in business. The only way a rival trader stayed in business was by people selling him fur.

Life in the community embraced activities other than attending to business. A bit of social life existed as well — within two weeks of my arrival, I had attended two dances and a weiner roast.

Physically, Churchill did not consist of one compact settlement. A rock formation, known as The Hill, divided the community into two sections. The Hudson's Bay Company store was located in one section, while the other section encompassed the traders. At six o'clock in the evening business ended and friendship commenced. The natural divider failed to prevent residents from both sections from mingling freely. At the weiner roast I met two female clerks from the trader's store.

The schoolhouse stood in close proximity to the Hudson's Bay Company store. By stacking the desks along a wall with the bench portions used as seats, the schoolhouse was converted into an excellent dance hall. Every Friday evening during the winter months, the desks were stacked against the wall; every Saturday morning they were returned to their normal positions. At these dances I soon became acquainted with the people who did their shopping at the trader's. Although square dances appeared in the program, they were interspersed with foxtrots, waltzes, polkas, two steps, and the latest dance fad called The Lambeth Walk. We tripped the light fantastic to such tunes as "Roll Out The Barrel," "Hang Out Our Washing On The Siegfried Line," and "Pocket Full Of Dreams."

One Sunday evening a local girl and myself decided to take advantage of the fine spring weather and go for a stroll along the railway tracks because they provided the smoothest pathway in the area. Since we had no definite destination in mind, we went sauntering along the trail the road bed provided. As we strode leisurely over the station platform, a trapper who had already possessed a pullman seat to ensure that he would be on the train when it left in the morning invited us aboard for a drink. He handed each of us a paper cup which he proceeded to fill with alcohol-fortified wine. He eagerly waited for a cup to be emptied, and immediately he refilled it to the overflow level. My companion soon began to pass her scarcely touched cup over to me. Since I had noticed that the first drink was poured from a gallon container that was already less than a quarter full, I estimated that our host's supply was almost exhausted. As a result, I had no qualms about keeping up this double drinking pace for the short period. I drastically underestimated my host.

After the gallon jug was emptied, the ingredients for mixing a fresh gallon were extracted from under the wicker seat. Although the quick-pouring trapper took an equal portion for himself each time he passed out a refill, he gave no indication that the amount of alcohol he could and would consume had any limit.

In the early hours of the morning the girl tired of her drunken companions. She decided to go home and we decided to escort her. She could walk; however, the trapper and myself resorted to crawling a good portion of the way. In case we needed further refreshment he carried a half-gallon of the concoction. We managed somehow to arrive at the girl's home without smashing the bottle. Neither of us wanted it and we left it on the kitchen table for the girl's father. Too much wine mixed with alcohol can sicken a person.

Above-normal temperatures blessed Churchill during the first week of July that summer. Consequently, I readily agreed to the suggestion from one of the unattached girls that we go for an after-dinner swim. At seven o'clock we hiked over the hill to the trader's store where one of the female clerks decided to expand our twosome into a foursome. Her efforts on the telephone found several young fellows eager to be her partner in other sports, but the idea of a dip in waters cooled by the ice fields in Hudson Bay appeared to leave them cold. The three of us continued the hike to the bank of the Churchill River. Since we wore bathing suits under our street clothes we were not embarassed over the lack of a bath house. However, we soon found that swimming enjoyment at Churchill was directly dependent on the tide. We experienced the frigid waters from the bay, although the rising tide had not yet reached its peak.

After proving to ourselves and to each other that we were not chicken, we jogged back to the traders. I also proved beyond all reasonable doubt to myself that although Churchill possessed a river beach, it fell far short of being an ideal swimming resort.

During the middle of July a ship anchored in the middle of the Churchill harbor. There were no communications advising the port authorities of the vessel's intended visit. When the crew and passengers came ashore they were viewed with apprehension. Soon, however, the tongue-loosening effect of the suds in the local tavern started one of them bragging about being a submarine commander in the German navy. The single RCMP officer was summoned, and he made certain that the entire company returned to their vessel.

Bob had served in World War One with the *Old Contemptables* and he had no intention of surrendering peacefully to a German invasion. He placed a loaded thirty-thirty rifle in the office where it stood ready for use by either of us, should it be required.

Within a couple of hours the harbors board established that the mystery ship, *The Continental*, was chartered by a movie company. Some of the shore visitors were actors, including the submarine commander. They were sailing to Wolstenholm to film a portion of *The 49th Parallel*. In order to pick up some additional cast members from the train station, they stopped over at Churchill. The additional cast failed to arrive and the ship resumed her journey without them.

The episode reinforced the concern of the townspeople. Since the beginning of the hostilities they felt that the harbor tied to a railway line running to the centre of the continent should not be left vulnerable to capture by an enemy nation. An enemy task force would have little difficulty in overcoming the resistance that one mounted policeman would provide.

The early autumn season in this northern area caused the ducks to begin traveling in migratory flocks during the latter part of August. This meant that the best duck-hunting period arrived early at Churchill. The general method of hunting closely resembled the one in use at York Factory, although the shooting location did not compare. At Churchill knolls on the mud flats served as waiting spots. In order to arrive at these knolls it was necessary to walk a couple of wearying miles in hip waders. Meanwhile, standing stationary, in order to not prematurely alarm the birds, failed to relieve the tiredness.

With the incoming tide, however, the birds flew overhead within shotgun range, and the excitement soon negated all my feelings of discomfort. I became so intent on my shooting successes, in fact, I neglected to notice the height of the incoming tide. Suddenly I found that in order to retrieve my birds, I had to wade in ice water deeper than the depth for which my hip waders were designed to protect me. Once they filled with ice water I realized the time had arrived for a decision. I could remain on the knoll, empty the hip waders and enjoy relative comfort until the tide rose another three feet. To avoid swimming to the firm land that bordered the mud flats I could remain on the knoll for the balance of the night. The decision was easy. I tied the birds to my waist and started for dry land. The two-mile walk in water-filled hip waders was as exhausting as walking twenty miles.

Production of neoprene and similar rubber synthetics had just entered its infancy. This meant that ninety-eight per cent of the footwear produced had leather soles, leaving the balance with rubber.

A formation of solid rock covered a large area and created an interesting part of the Churchill landscape. I soon learned that walking over this rock formation, uncushioned by any form of foliage, was being unkind to one's feet. A half-hour stroll resulted in foot blisters and bruises. Sore feet could be avoided if one had the foresight, and the necessary source of supply, to first equip oneself with a pair of foam-rubber-soled shoes. After my first hike over the rocky terrain, I realized why Bob decided to stock this unusual type of footwear in several sizes.

The local residents wore this footwear or avoided walking over the rocks. When an annual excursion train arrived full of passengers, these tourists were totally unaware of the discomfort of walking over the rocks without proper footwear. Many of them learned by experience. The inclusive packaged holiday included a tour of the port in operation. To accomplish this the train arrived while the *Nascopie* was loading, thereby ensuring that the station warehouse was empty. The climax of the seaport visit consisted of a dance held in the empty warehouse. We locals were able to enjoy the dancing, but a good portion of the tourists found that the condition of their feet forced them to treat this northern shindig as strictly a spectator sport.

Although one community center would have been sufficient to serve the village population, two centers existed. A bunkhouse from the harbor construction days provided an alternative to the school house. The bunkhouse, with the bunks and other unnecessary equipment removed, stood in the general vicinity of the trader's store.

Although it was the larger hall of the two it was seldom used, possibly due to the need of obtaining permission from some federal government authority. The final sailing of the *Nascopie* coincided with the conclusion of port activities for the year. This windup occasion warranted seeking the special permission, and authorization arrived to hold a dance in this hall at the last moment.

During the festivities a couple of my drinking buddies for the evening called a hasty conference. It appeared we had exhausted our supply of liquid refreshment. One of these fellows offered to replenish the supply with a couple of bottles he had at home so we piled into the Hudson Bay Company truck to make the necessary trek to this oasis.

The twelve-year-old vehicle showed signs of old age. The wiring system no longer functioned as efficiently as it once had. A thirty-degree or greater turn of the steering wheel caused the lights to extinguish. We had to quickly turn the wheel back so that connections would re-establish and the lights would again illuminate the road. Providing the road was sufficiently wide, cornering in this zig-zag fashion had obvious advantages over driving in the dark. The trail from the dance hall to the cabin twisted its way through a series of mansion-sized boulders. While negotiating one of these turns, my quick return twist of the wheel caused the truck to climb one of these boulders. We lifted the vehicle back onto the trail and were relieved to see that no apparent damage had been done to the running gear. But a new symptom of old age became immediately apparent — the vehicle could no longer hold its water.

Although Bob never mentioned the incident to me, I suspect it was the final goof that prompted the Hudson's Bay Company to make the port-closing wingding my Churchill farewell gathering as well. Two days later I found myself on the *Nascopie,* heading for Chesterfield Inlet where she was to rendezvous with the *Fort Severn.* The *Fort Severn* was to furnish my passage to Repulse Bay.

I had grown so accustomed to the night life at Churchill that the thought of departing did not leave me overjoyed. I envisioned the life of isolation I would lead at Repulse Bay and reached a rapid conclusion. I would sever my connections with the Hudson's Bay Company. I would have no difficulty obtaining a well-paying job on the outside because most of the men my age were fighting in the war. The fact that I had twice been found medically unfit for military service would now be in my favor. My list of qualifications would include a rejection slip. I counted up my salary credits. I didn't owe my soul to the company store; I merely owed them four dollars and seventy-five cents. My daydream ended. It would require a more favorable balance to pay my fare to Winnipeg and the offer to continue my apprenticeship at Repulse Bay became an offer I could not refuse.

I went further into debt by purchasing shaving accessories, the entire stock of 120 camera film (four rolls) and other necessities. By the time I'd completed my shopping I'd spent my salary for two months in advance. My limited wardrobe made packing easy and soon my preparations for the journey were completed. So, with a bulging packsack on one shoulder and a huge chip on the other, I boarded the *Nascopie*.

To the
Unfriendly Arctic

The calm sea and the balanced cargo in the vessel's hold should have produced a relaxing trip to Chesterfield Inlet. However, my emergency supplies at Churchill included an unopened bottle of scotch whiskey and since I did not consider my departure from Manitoba's seaport an occasion for celebration, I wrapped it with a suit jacket and stowed it near the bottom of my packsack. A couple of Hudson's Bay Company men were returning to their arctic outposts and apparently smelled this supply. They descended on my cabin with the intention of throwing an impromptu party with my booze. My immediate reaction was to throw them out as briskly as they had entered. Unfortunately, I hesitated for a moment, giving them the opportunity to commiserate with me. We were all in the same boat; only the outposts where we were to serve our isolation differed. Misery loves sympathy. Sometime after midnight when the last drop left my bottle, my sympathetic friends left my stateroom. I never saw either of them again.

Long before daylight the noise of the ship's anchor dropping awakened me. I pulled the blankets around me a little tighter, rolled over and went back to sleep. But my dream of disembarking at Chesterfield relaxed and well-rested was not to be. At the first sign of the dawn breaking, the Chesterfield post manager sent his assistant to summon me to the beach. He brusquely told me that they expected me to do my share of the stevedoring chores. I answered with a silent sneer and, after adjusting the chip on my shoulder to the correct angle, picked up my baggage and accompanied him to the staff house.

At the house I was shown to my room. I changed to suitable garb for my assigned task and found my way back to the kitchen. The post manager felt that delivering a speech of welcome to me was an important function. Rather than welcome me at the scene of the action he instead took up a position with his back absorbing the warmth from the kitchen range, permitting an easy view of the door through which I would enter. My appearance served as his cue. He took up a position in the middle of the floor and began delivering an obviously well-rehearsed speech. He explained how shiptime meant that all apprentices should get with it and work if they wished to remain employed with the company. I yawned, stretched and asked no one in particular, "What if they do not wish to remain in the company's employ?"

Without answering, he offered me breakfast. I spurned his offer and found my way to the beach. Although assisting with the unloading would have enabled me to keep warmer, I stood around joking and chatting with the clerk who was about to leave Chesterfield on furlough. From a distance the assistant observed our lack of active participation and rushed over to hold a hasty consultation with the manager. Their attitudes toward me were the only indication of the result of this consultation that I received. During the balance of my three-day stay at Chesterfield, the post manager always offered me the usual "good morning" pleasantries. The assistant never spoke to me again.

In the latter stages of summer I'd made the acquaintance of the carpenter constructing the warehouse for the Hudson's Bay Company at Churchill. Since he worked by contract rather than by the hour, he was not reluctant to work through the long summer evenings. Long after I'd swallowed the last bite of my evening meal he could still be found on the project. He considered the ability to read the rafter and brace scales on his carpenter's square a major accomplishment, possibly because he had limited formal education. He spent several evenings explaining how he used these scales and listed the people he'd met who did not have the smallest clue of the ways these important angle measurements were used.

When he finished the building at Churchill and left to construct one at Chesterfield, I am certain my name was added to his list of dunderheads that were too stupid to read a carpenter's square. But whether my name appeared on the top, the bottom, or not on the list at all did not matter. His face showed obvious pleasure when he saw me easing my way through the skeleton of the building he was now working on. Not only was he happy to see me, I was happy to see him. By using my layover time visiting with him I could avoid further strain on the relationship between myself and the local Hudson's Bay Company staff.

If any truth exists in the theory that it takes three days for a cold to develop, then my final hectic days at Churchill caught up with me at Chesterfield. A head cold added to my miseries — my head swam, my eyes watered, and my nose brimmed over. When the Fort Severn arrived, one of the crew members took it upon himself to advise me that it would be just as easy to feel miserable at Repulse Bay as anywhere else. These words of wisdom did little to ease my misery as I boarded the vessel, especially since the head cold now topped my list of unwanted possessions.

Originally, sails provided the only motive power for the Fort Severn. At a later date some of the cargo capacity space was sacrificed to provide for an engine room. The schooner's main source of power now consisted of a diesel engine. However, the masts still stretched skyward and the sails lay neatly folded at strategic points around the deck. When ideal wind conditions were available, the Fort Severn could be quickly converted back to a sailing vessel. A rough ride by diesel power could be converted to a smooth ride by sail. Unfortunately, when travelling north, ideal conditions for using sails seldom prevailed and this trip proved to be no exception. Three hours after leaving Chesterfield I got rid of my head cold. I traded it for a case of sea sickness and I received the worst part of the trade. My only consolation existed in the fact that I now had company — two priests and a bishop belonging to the order of Mary the Immaculate, completed the ship's passenger list. The choppy ride appeared to cause them greater discomfort than it caused me.

During the vessel's unloading stops at York Factory and the time spent loading at Churchill, I'd made the acquaintance of several crew members from the Fort Severn. To avoid being an absolute loner during the voyage, I decided to renew these acquaintances. The small amount of reading I had done on the subject of ships comprised my entire knowledge of a sailor's duties. The only seafaring duty I could assist with was the cooking; even a landlubber learns something about food.

The cook did not acquire his culinary expertise through the use of a cook book. His schooling had ended before he mastered the art of reading and rather than admit to this handicap, he made every possible effort to camouflage it. His favorite ruse consisted of voicing slight variations of the question, "Now where did I put that tin of peas? I had it in my hand just a minute ago."

Even though little more than dry toast would remain in my squeamish stomach, I followed advice from the adage, "never offend the cook." Long before we arrived at our destination I developed a conditioned reflex to his repeated question. I would look among the canned vegetables, find a can of peas and hand it to him saying, "Here it is. You must have put it back in the box."

One morning I was awakened by the sounds of feverish activity on the deck above. The crewman who had started his watch at midnight could not be found. Although the wheel had been latched tight the ship had strayed from her course. The eerie sound of keel scraping the ocean floor could be clearly heard. The possibility of the vessel beaching herself on an arctic island shore and all on board becoming disaster statistics bordered on becoming a reality. After a few hectic minutes spent coaxing the schooner into deeper waters, we began a search for the missing crewman. One of his mates found him sleeping soundly in the folds of a canvas sail. For the balance of the trip, relations were not cordial between the over-relaxed sailor and the remaining crew members. He had travelled these waters with the *Fort Severn* crew every season for the past ten years but this voyage on the vessel proved to be his last. His familiarity with arctic waters and contempt for the hazards encountered when sailing were not universally shared by others in the same boat.

The surrounding islands and their shallow shorelines made the passage sufficiently treacherous to provide me with all the excitement my nervous system required. Huge cakes of ice bobbing around in the water now added to this excitement. Their addition changed what might have been a thrilling experience to a terrifying one. The further north we progressed, the more prevalent these floes became. Eventually the helmsman found it necessary to ease the vessel through whatever narrow channels of open water he could find.

I had been assigned to the front bunk in the fo'c'sle. The sound of plank scraping against ice did not permit me to drop off to sleep without a worry in the world. Since I noticed the planks bending with the pressure several times, any sleep I did manage had its full quota of nightmares.

As we neared the mouth of Repulse Bay we were within close proximity to the north magnetic pole. Although the shoreline assured us that we were still travelling in a northern direction, the compass needle indicated we were travelling almost due west. On one side the rocky shoreline stood waiting and willing to wreck our craft, while on the other a mass of floating ice constantly threatened to drive us onto that rocky shore. Often, smaller cakes broke free from the mother floe and forced the helmsman to swerve abruptly to avoid hitting them head on. For a novice like myself, the experience proved to be more than a bit scary. I can easily understand why Henry Hudson's men mutinied.

On the morning of the third day after leaving Chesterfield, a member of the crew shook me awake. He had some mistaken idea that if I missed any details of the forbidding shoreline as we entered the mouth of Repulse Bay I would never forgive myself. During the night a west wind had augmented the efforts of the outgoing tide and freed the channel from ice floes while a light fog limited visibility to approximately a quarter mile. Since the fluctuating compass needle made visual navigation mandatory, seeing the shoreline became absolutely necessary. Just beyond that curtain of mist I am certain that the floating mass of ice lay in ambush, waiting for a change in the wind so that it could again resume its game of cat and mouse with the venturesome vessel. But my fears of a forced fight for survival in the icy waters of the arctic soon ended when the buildings of Repulse Bay loomed through the mist.

The fog lifted as the anchor dropped. Set in a valley surrounded on three sides by rocky hills, stood a house, a detached shed and the Hudson's Bay Company store. A few tattered skin tents stood between the house and the shoreline while a solid sheet of ice covered the shaded hillside of a gully behind the store. The ice provided the only relief from the pebbles, stones, boulders and sheets of bedrock that constituted the landscape. One glance was sufficient to support my preconceived idea; Repulse Bay was desolate.

Because of a resolution not to shave until some situation warranted that I should look my best, I'd left my razor packed since leaving Churchill. The only disembarking preparation I intended to make consisted of adjusting the chip I still carried on my shoulder. But I never really completed my planned preparations.

How do you adjust a shoulder chip while your hand is vigorously pumped by the chap who is to be your companion for the next year? How can you use a cynical sneer to reply to a smile of welcome that covers the entire width of the wearer's face? Before the last waves of the dropped anchor ebbed away, Tom Crawford, the post manager at Repulse Bay, had climbed aboard to welcome me.

"I'll say hello to the district manager," he said, "and then we'll go ashore."

A Friendly Acquaintance

In a manner somewhat shyer than that of her husband, Mrs. Crawford extended a welcome every bit as warm. I remembered that while they were worming the next drink from my bottle of booze, the two Hudson's Bay Company men I met on the *Nascopie* had gone to great lengths to warn me that Mrs. Crawford was part Eskimo. I never understood the need for this warning. Certainly the girl in question was born and raised in the arctic and spoke the native tongue as fluently as she spoke English. But if her personality and character traits were a result of the mixture of true Canadian blood in her veins, then the Red Cross should start developing the same mixture for their blood banks. People with Mrs. Crawford's personality and characteristics are far too few.

After my formal introduction to Winnie Crawford, we returned to the store where a growing pile of trade goods occupied the center of the warehouse floor. Tom explained that since the natives were more than capable of doing the necessary lifting and heaving, it would be totally unnecessary for either of us to get involved with the more strenuous portion of the unloading chore. All we needed to do was to verify the bills of lading. I found the number on the box, bundle or bale, called it out and Tom crossed it off the sheet. We carried the few perishables that were brought in for the staff mess to the residence pantry. The balance of the cargo lay scattered and heaped into piles wherever the natives had seen fit to dump their loads. After the schooner departed, ample time was available for sorting and storing.

During my previous visit to the Crawford household, their fourteen-month-old daughter was too busy napping to pay any attention to intruding strangers but now the toddler was very much awake.

To make certain he heard the latest war news, Tom switched on the radio as soon as we entered the room. Soon the warm-up hum gave way to strains of "Oh Johnny How You Can Love". This gave the baby sufficient time to decide that she would accept me. Possibly because her father was involved in a discussion with a couple of natives in the kitchen, she held out her hands to be picked up and I danced around the room a couple of times with her in my arms. The news announcer's voice interrupted the dance music and I lowered the infant to the floor. She ran to occupy her usual spot on her father's lap. Obviously I would share my period of isolation with a family that readily accepted me. As soon as I had caught up on the news, I shaved off my dirty, itchy beard.

We sat up late that night while Tom and the district manager went over the past year's business records. Several times I heard the name Wager Inlet mentioned. Judging by the context in which the name was mentioned I realized that Wager served as an outpost under the control of Repulse Bay. However, no evidence existed of an outpost manager waiting to pick up his trade goods.

By daybreak the next morning the *Fort Severn* had departed for Igloolik. In the early afternoon another vessel appeared in the harbor and Tom immediately remarked, "Ah there's that Peterhead from Wager."

The boat anchored and I received my introduction to Wager Dick. Some time later I realized that Peterhead was the name of a type of boat, rather than a name Tom used to describe an inept outpost trader. Dick was a full-blooded Eskimo and, although I'm certain he had an Eskimo name, I never heard it used. Even his fellow natives spoke of him as Dick or Wager Dick. His position as outpost manager automatically gave Dick the position of ship's captain. His brother made up the crew. Following the Eskimo custom of family togetherness, both captain and crew were accompanied by their wives and families.

Dick's family consisted of his wife and two children. The occidental features of the children, a girl of fourteen and her slightly younger brother, provided ample evidence that men other than Dick had kept warm during the long winter evenings by snuggling up to the mother. I later learned that this woman was not the only wife in Dick's life. In the past he was husband to three wives.

However, the influence of the missionaries and the problems of providing for a large family had persuaded Dick to practice monogamy. Consequently, he found single husbands for two of his wives and retained the third. Being a man of sound business sense, he retained the wife whose experiences with two white men assured her of an income. There were no trains, buses or other forms of mass transportation that would enable a person to leave Repulse for parts unknown.

The whereabouts of the fathers of these children was well known and, although the possibility of legal action was not too great, both men avoided the possibility by providing support for the youngsters.

Dick's brother had one wife and one child whose features gave every indication that his ancestry was solely native.

Without any trace of emotion Dick explained in picturesque, rather than perfect English, the reason for his late arrival. A badly worn bearing caused the boat motor to start hammering so they anchored in the shelter of an island. Here, they fashioned a new bearing shell from a walrus tusk. This improvisation repaired the ailing engine and when they arrived at Repulse, not even the faintest sound of a bearing malfunction could be heard.

Once the formal introductions and greetings had been completed, the next order of business consisted of reviewing the Wager Inlet records. Because it afforded Dick an opportunity to display his natural gift of pantomime, he enjoyed record keeping. He began by withdrawing a case from his pocket, opening up the case and extracting a pair of circular-lensed glasses. These he carefully cleaned with a piece of dirty rag before adjusting the spectacles on his nose at the right angle that would permit easy vision over the top of the rims.

All the transactions the outpost handled during the year were listed in neatly spelled-out Eskimo syllabics. Amounts were noted in arabic numerals. Schools did not exist in that part of the country, so Dick was obviously a self-educated man. Since his only exposure to English consisted of his contact with white traders, the writing feat could be called nothing less than remarkable. Keeping written records was a custom employed only by the white men. Any records the natives found necessary to keep, such as the object that marked a turn in the trail, were committed to memory and passed on by word of mouth.

As Dick went over his transactions for last year, Tom paid little attention to the details. He contented himself with writing English names over the Eskimo syllabics, then carefully listing all the goods Dick was to take for the coming season's trade. As he explained the list, the native wrote the Eskimo names in the syllabics of his own language over the English titles.

After Dick returned to Wager, I was assigned the task of auditing the records he left behind. Marking the value of the fox pelts presented no problem because, regardless of the quality, a fixed price per pelt was allowed. But pricing the trade goods proved to be a part-time exercise that spread out over the next three weeks. When I finished, I realized why my senior staff member gave little attention to Dick's accounting efforts. Dick used a simple and functional format and everything balanced to the penny. Now the records had to be transcribed to the complicated balance sheet used by the head office accountants.

There was no great need to complete the storing and sorting of trade goods within a certain time limit. But procuring fresh food for the coming winter had to be undertaken whenever the opportunity presented itself. Consequently, when a flock of about 300 ptarmigan landed within five hundred yards of the post, I found myself immediately dispatched to find a case of twenty-two shells.

When I returned with a thousand rounds of ammunition, Tom handed me a rifle. He picked up an identical weapon for himself and we began walking towards the birds. We approached to within thirty-five yards of the birds, knelt on the bare rock and fired one shot each. The flock took wing and flew for approximately three hundred yards where a mossy bank, exposed to the full warmth of the midday sun, made an excellent landing field for the ptarmigan.

This time we managed to fire a couple of rounds each before the flock again took off. But like their relatives I met at York Factory, these birds did not believe in embarking on a full flight retreat until they were certain it was absolutely essential for their survival. They again landed within rifle range. This time we crept up on our quarry until we reached point-blank range. Tom suggested I take up a comfortable firing position lying down, cautioning me to fire only at the birds on the outer edge of the group because the fluttering of a wounded bird in the midst of the feeding flock would frighten the entire assembly into taking flight. His strategy proved to be the proper one. We bagged over seventy ptarmigan before the wiser members of the flock decided something was not quite right. They took flight in a northern direction, turning one hundred and eighty degrees, and flew back high over our heads. It seems that even a bird-brained ptarmigan not only knew better than to spend the winter at Repulse Bay, but also had the ability to employ the safest way to get to a more southern region.

Our game almost filled our packsacks. We carried it home and placed it on the deck of an abandoned Peterhead boat where it would be safe. Nature's deep freeze was already in operation. The dogs could not reach the birds and the Eskimos did not steal. In January we were still enjoying an occasional ptarmigan meal.

The abandoned ship, whose deck served as a natural freezer, sat in a gully beside the store. The easiest though longest way from the vessel to the house followed a trail that passed between the store and the shore. As soon as we reached a portion of the path that allowed us a clear view of the harbor, Tom noticed a small boat riding at anchor. Where the vessel's name might have been once, nothing remained but signs of peeling paint. Several dogs were looking longingly over the gunnels at the distant shore. We assumed that some affluent natives were paying the post a visit. Mrs. Crawford told us that the visitors were Mr. and Mrs. Tom Manning, the last members of the British Canadian Arctic Expedition to leave the arctic.

Since they found no one home at the Hudson's Bay post they went to visit the mission. Soon after our return they again knocked on the door. The Mannings were racing the elements in an effort to reach Churchill before the winter's ice prevented them from traveling by boat.

Since a portion of the British Canadian Arctic Expedition had spent a period at Repulse Bay, Manning was well aware of the two-way radio equipment at the post. His concern over some of the specimens he had shipped from Igloolik in the *Fort Severn* was so great that he felt it warranted taking the time to travel the extra thirty miles to send radio instructions regarding the disposition of the specimens upon arrival. I managed to reach the control station and Mr. Manning sent his message. They stayed for dinner and delayed their departure after dinner long enough to allow me to write a letter home. Mrs. Manning assured me it would be posted as soon as they reached civilization.

Because of their desire for an early departure they chose to spend the night on their tiny vessel. Although we arose before daylight the next morning, we found that the Mannings had already left. A week later ice began to cover the bay and Tom remarked that the Mannings would never reach Churchill by boat. He was right. The letter that left Repulse in September arrived at Souris in late January of the following year.

The accuracy of the rifle I used for the ptarmigan slaughter impressed me so much that I immediately offered to purchase it from Tom. The weapon was not for sale. The Crawfords received matching rifles for a wedding present. The one I used belonged to Mrs. Crawford. She gave me permission to use it for the remainder of my stay at Repulse and since it was a no-cost, interest-free loan, I certainly had no argument with that arrangement.

Before leaving Churchill I had taken advantage of a fresh shipment of underwear and purchased several pairs. This proved fortunate because this type of apparel was not stocked at Repulse Bay. People living in igloos did not bother with Saturday night baths and there was little need to change into clean clothes. If undergarments were available to the natives they would wear them for a year, then new garments would be pulled on without removing the old garment first. Eventually the dirty, rotting cloth, clinging to their bodies far more closely than their own animal-hide clothing, would begin to disease their skin. The government took the easiest solution to the problem; rather than teaching the natives to change their undies, they made it illegal to sell such garments to the Eskimos.

But a suitable wardrobe to withstand the continuous frigid weather throughout the Repulse Bay winters consisted of more than a few changes of underwear. My unlined duck parka would prove useless in an arctic blizzard. Fortunately, the stock that was unloaded from the *Fort Severn* included a bale of caribou-skin parkas, tanned and sewn by the natives at Eskimo Point. They came in various sizes and I had my pick of the bale. With little difficulty I found one that provided a far better fit than my previous custom-tailored, duck effort from Gillam.

I had believed my York Factory moccasins with their duffle linings would be suitable footwear for Repulse Bay but the Crawfords felt differently. Not only did they feel I needed better footwear, they did something about it. As if by magic, a pair of sealskin boots with duffle stockings appeared in my room. When I enquired about who and how much I should pay my questions remained unanswered. I knew that duffle was carried in the store; we sold it by the linear yard. But sealskin was certainly not part of the store stock. The native customers had as much need to purchase sealskin as they had to purchase ice in the wintertime.

During their stay at Repulse, members of the British Canadian Arctic Expedition were allowed full use of the two-way radio. However, the communication equipment was not installed to benefit modern-day explorers. The Hudson's Bay Company selected Repulse as one of the first radio-equipped posts because of its remote location and the one-in-four chance that the supply ship would find it impossible to complete the journey.

The equipment consisted of a six-volt power plant, a transmitter suitable for transmitting Morse code, and a receiver equipped with earphones instead of a speaker. Even with the low supply of voltage power, it proved more than adequate to reach the control station at Chesterfield Inlet. In fact, radio reception was so good at Repulse, we were able to pick up European standard broadcast stations, including the German propaganda station which was unquestionably beamed at the British Isles.

As Tom never had the opportunity to learn Morse code, my arrival at Repulse meant that he now had someone to help him practise. Soon we were contacting not only the control station at Chesterfield, but several other radio-equipped posts as well. Before Christmas we joined a gossip club that stretched the entire length of Hudson Bay.

Although the primary purpose of installing a radio at Repulse was to provide a means of communication between the post and the head office in Winnipeg, a fringe benefit soon developed. The post manager at Eskimo Point expressed a willingness to handle our personal messages. I spent many hours tapping out Morse code communications to Eskimo Point. The post manager, in turn, typed out the letters, addressed them and started them on their way to Churchill by dog team express. We did not get overnight delivery.

During the dog team travel season, the monthly return train schedule linked Churchill to The Pas. Consequently, after the letter arrived at Churchill there was reasonable assurance that within the next couple of months it would reach the area of regular mail service. But even the three-month wait for an answer was a big improvement over the annual supply ship delivery.

A fringe benefit I personally derived from the radio equipment was the aid it provided in my efforts to become a touch typist. The Repulse Bay library included an instruction book on typing. The author of the book had gone into great detail and explained that in order to be a good typist, good health and regular exercise were a necessity. It listed bicycling as an excellent method of keeping fit. Even though the book was not written with a student in a remote arctic trading post in mind, it covered the important items of touch typing. It explained which fingers should strike which keys and contained the necessary fingering exercises to ensure that the fingering process became automatic. The radio receiver headphones deadened all sound other than the whistles of the dots and dashes. As a result, my mind was not distracted by the clatter of the typewriter keys. Once I mastered the fingering, typing from the radio came easy. The Morse code spelled out one letter at a time and my mind concentrated on interpreting that letter. By listening to the commercial news casts I soon found myself able to type at speeds in excess of thirty words per minute. Such a speed fell short of that which was required to qualify me as a top-grade stenographer, but it was certainly sufficient to produce legible copy faster than it could be produced by my scrawly, scribbly handwriting.

Repulse Bay teems with history. It is unfortunate that very little of this history was ever recorded in writing as it happened. However, written records are not necessary when indisputable evidence exists in other forms. About three miles from the post buildings stood the remains of stone and sod shelters. Prior to my arrival at Repulse Bay, members of the British Canadian Arctic Expedition had spent several months studying the remains of these long-abandoned dwellings. By carefully sweeping a layer of dust from the floor a fraction of an inch at a time, they established that at least a thousand years had passed since the dwellings were last used. Remnants of similar dwellings remained in the northern portions of Siberia and Alaska as well as Canada, leading to the deduction that man migrated from Asia many centuries ago. To me, even the idea of primitive man migrating from some other part of the globe to Repulse was questionable. With the climate and physical attractions the eastern arctic had to offer, it would have made more sense if the migration had been in the opposite direction — but then, I've never spent time in Siberia.

The archaeologists also passed along a few other bits of information to Tom, and he passed them on to me. The houses were originally built on the shoreline. Now, even at high tide, they stood about one hundred and fifty feet back from the water's edge; I readily accepted this as proof that the oceans are constantly shrinking.

By law, these historic sites could be disturbed by no one except a qualified anthropologist or archaeologist. The natives, lacking the Cambridge degrees held by members of the British Canadian Arctic Expedition, lived by the laws of survival. The floors of these ancient houses provided an excellent source of earth for fashioning mud shoes for sleigh runners. When a person's mind is focused on the need to obtain food for the immediate future, he worries little about what his ancestors ate thousands of winters in the past. They merely take the good earth where they find it.

Most human settlements will deplete the supply of game animals in their immediate vicinity over a period of time. It is assumed that these original colonies of stone houses were no exception. The colonists found it necessary to travel to locate the animals they depended on for food. As a result, they developed the art of constructing skin tents and snow houses. Both types of dwelling permitted speedy erection and the skin tents were portable. The permanent shelters of the early settlers were abandoned and the villages became primitive ghost towns.

On the larger islands that dotted Repulse Bay, scattered remains of rock shelters were found. Whalers from around the world constructed these shelters to protect them from the wind. Even during the summer months a breeze chilled by the ice floes and frigid waters of the Arctic Ocean is so unpleasantly cool, it can turn a person's face blue and make his teeth chatter. Apart from these wind shelters, the high points of the islands provided a firmness not found at the top of a ship's mast. But perhaps due to the short supply of the mammals, whaling in these waters was abandoned several years prior to my arrival. The natural elements were already erasing all traces of these original shelters. However, the features of some of the local natives provided non-erasable evidence that visitors from around the world enjoyed hospitable favors from the native women. I had no difficulty in discerning Nordic, negroid and Portuguese features in the faces of several of the Inuit.

Similar to the policy of the other stores in the Hudson's Bay Company chain, the Repulse Bay store remained locked when not occupied. However, unlike the other posts at which I was stationed, there seemed to be no obvious reason for keeping it locked. The thought of thievery never entered the Eskimo mind.

When an Eskimo family reached the post on a trading venture, they brought their fox catch directly to the post house. Usually the trapped foxes were frozen stiff before the natives found them and subsequently had to be at least partially thawed before they could be skinned. The natives had no method for thawing their catches, resulting in the offer of frozen, unskinned carcasses for trading sticks. A trading stick had a monetary value of fifty cents. A fox pelt, regardless of quality, had a flat value of ten dollars. We counted the carcasses and advised the trapper how many trading sticks he would receive for his catch. Once the natives knew how much they had to spend, they visited in the kitchen with the natives who camped in the immediate area.

Trading, Repluse Bay style, consisted of more than making a few purchases in the company store. Trading consisted of, among other things, a big kettle of tea on the kitchen stove and a good supply of hardtack on the kitchen table. The biscuit and tea period was not merely a frill added locally. It was the custom at all Eskimo trading posts. This tradition probably originated when the Revillon Freres competed with the Hudson's Bay Company for the Inuit business, since the way to an Inuit's heart and business was through his stomach. Natives have been known to switch their allegiance between the Anglican and Catholic missions, depending upon which mission provided the greatest abundance of tea and hardtack. The pelt counting, visiting, etc., all took place in the Hudson's Bay Company house. The store had no heat and was frequented only when natives arrived to trade. A period of six weeks to two months could pass without either of us going near the store.

After an hour spent drinking tea, chewing on hardtack, and visiting, the family with money to spend announced their readiness to ascertain which items they would spend it on. We unlocked the store; the buyers separated from the socializers and wandered, unattended through the store and warehouse complex making mental notes of the available items they required. When they considered their purchasing power large enough, they made their decision as to the available items they would like to have. Once the temporarily affluent natives decided which items to purchase, Tom and myself were summoned from the house. The non-traders remained in the house and continued with the social gathering until the last mug of tea had been gulped and the last biscuit bolted.

The stacks of trading sticks were placed on the counter and the shopping commenced. The man of the family assumed the role of official shopper. Invariably, a tin of tobacco was the first item purchased; trading immediately halted while all our customers rolled cigarettes. (Everybody smoked.) From inside the folds of their parkas the women produced cigarette holders. An infant, carried in the pouch that was sewn into the back of the mother's parka, shared the cigarette with the mother. Frequently the same infant would be breastfed a little later. As soon as everyone had lit a cigarette, trading resumed. Family conferences became frequent as shopping progressed, not to determine what to buy but rather, what quantity. Their needs had to be balanced against the dwindling stock of trade sticks. The spending of the last stick did not necessarily mean the end of trading because discussions and adjustments followed in earnest. A pound of tea would be returned and three sticks placed back on the counter which might then be used to purchase chewing gum or some of the small stock of chocolate bars we carried. Occasionally, a second tin of tobacco would be exchanged for a pound of tea. Regardless of their last minute needs, Tom nor myself were never approached for any appreciable amount of credit. On some occasions, the purchase of a major item, such as a pair of sled runners, necessitated carrying an outstanding portion of the payment in the company books. Whenever this happened, the native in question insisted on paying the debt in full at the first opportunity. The next visit the native made to the post, sufficient foxes were placed in a heap to cover the debt before the actual trading carcasses were produced.

One of Tom's predecessors extended a native three fox pelts' worth of credit. For some reason, three years elapsed before the native made his next trip back to Repulse. During the interim, the value of fur had risen considerably, due to the war. Two and one quarter pelts would now cover this advance, but no amount of explanation from Tom would persuade the native that he owed less than three foxes.

Trading was not an everyday occurrence. Frequently as much as six weeks would elapse without a customer setting foot inside the store. Consequently, no facilities for heating the building existed and the temperature behind the counter was only slightly higher than that of the great outdoors.

The natives developed a type of skin clothing that provided the best type of insulation to protect their bodies from the cold, but used only unlined sealskin mitts to protect their hands. I tried a pair of these mitts during the first warning that winter was near. My cold fingers gave me sufficient reason to consider them a poor substitute for the duffle-lined gauntlets I acquired at Gillam. I wore my heavier and warmer mitts during the trading sessions in the company store.

From Tom I learned that there are systems of recording trading transactions employed by various traders that do not include freezing any fingers. The most common of these systems consists of committing the details to memory. Later, in the comfort of the post living room, the details were entered in the ledger. I lacked sufficient confidence in my memory to attempt this method and made a few quick notes on a piece of scrap paper instead, quickly returning my cold, naked hand to the cozy warmth of the duffle. This may possibly have had some bearing on the name *Teegaracktee*, the name by which the natives referred to me. It translates into "He who writes."

As well as providing a meeting place for the Inuit, and serving the normal function that its name implies, the kitchen also provided a workshop for the Eskimo chore boy. The native's prime function consisted of skinning the fox carcasses and scraping the fat from the skins. In addition to several other odd jobs around the post, he served as the official native welcoming committee because his work location ensured he would be on hand whenever any trading party arrived. He talked the most, laughed the most, ate the most hardtack, and drank the most tea. The influence of the mission had converted him to the Christian faith and he was baptized and given the name Peter.

Peter enjoyed his fox-skinning chores. He carefully scrutinized the fat he scraped from the pelts, sometimes throwing it into a slop pail, sometimes throwing it into his mouth. These tidbits he gummed with obvious delight. Peter had lived the required number of years to place a white man in the middle-age group and an Eskimo in the senior citizenship class. He inevitably received the name "Old Peter." Since another elderly native had also been baptized Peter, the Hudson's Bay Company chore boy was better known as "Old Peter the Fox Skinner." This name followed the Eskimo practice of naming people for some unique occupation or physical characteristic. Names such as Gabby, Slim or the Storekeep that would have been acceptable as nicknames in English, proved acceptable in every way in Inuit. I suspect the name Peter was used merely as a courtesy when they spoke with the local white people.

The other Peter, "Old Peter The Hunter," lived with his son and daughter-in-law. Since the family never ventured far from the post, they were classified as post Eskimos. However, they obtained far more of their food from hunting and fishing than they did from the handouts and mugups at the mission and Hudson's Bay Company.

One evening Mrs. Crawford informed us that Peter had shot

himself. He found that he could no longer do his fair share when he accompanied a hunting party. While travelling on one of the little islands that was five miles distant from the shore, he requested a loaded rifle and half an hour's solitude. Although the son knew the purpose the old man had in mind, he granted his father's final request. When the party returned they found Peter sitting against a rock with the rifle barrel still in his mouth. They removed the gun and left the old man in his sitting position, piling up rocks to form a suitable tomb. Peter picked a spot that would enable him to look out over the sea for eternity and there they would permit him to remain.

Peter the Fox Skinner was not the only native helper around the post. A much younger chap, "Albert's Boy," spent a great deal of his time functioning as an outside chore boy. I seldom heard his native name, which sounded like Aluk. But since Tom spoke of him as Albert's Boy, I used that name as well, because I could speak and remember it without difficulty.

Albert's Boy was accustomed to being with white men and although he now associated freely with the Hudson's Bay Company staff, at one time he was part of their opposition. He was a crew member on a supply ship used by the Revillon Freres.

The Revillon Freres was one of the few companies which, during the past several decades, managed to offer some noticeable competition to the Bay. However, the Hudson's Bay Company successfully eliminated this competition by purchasing the rival company and all its assets. Among other things, the company assets provided the Bay with two sets of buildings at Repulse. The premises formerly occupied by the Revillon Freres were donated to the Catholic mission. Since two vessels were no longer necessary to visit and service one company's posts, Albert's Boy became a retired sailor. His exposure to the Kabloona way of life made him an excellent handyman around the post.

During the ten to fifteen years that Tom spent in the Arctic he acquired several possessions that made life in remote areas more enjoyable. Two of the more important possessions were a canoe equipped with an outboard motor and a dog team. These two items provided the only non-commercial methods of transportation between Churchill and the North Pole.

To ensure that a supply of fresh meat would always be available, the dog team was mandatory. Tom and Albert's Boy owned a good team between them; each owned some of the dogs outright, while two pups were owned jointly. The dogs had to be fed and one of the best sources of dog food was seal meat. I soon received instructions in the most prolific method of obtaining the necessary meat. The method began with launching Tom's canoe, sailing several miles into Repulse Bay and plucking the seals from the water. Before the seals could be plucked, they had to be shot.

The season when the arctic waters are free from ice is extremely short. The days suitable for hunting seal during this short season are few and far between. Without a perfectly calm sea, any attempt to shoot and harpoon a seal would have a good chance of failing. Before the bay froze over, Tom took advantage of every suitable day and obtained a good supply of seal meat. He seemed to have a built-in weather radar. Several mornings he woke me at three o'clock in order to launch the canoe and arrive at a good seal-hunting area by daylight. Due to some sixth sense, Albert's Boy was always on hand to help with the launching chores when we arrived at the warehouse-store complex that also served as a boatshed.

Any properly organized seafaring vessel has a spot assigned for each member of the crew and Tom's canoe was properly organized. Albert's Boy sat in the front of the small craft ready to do the harpooning, while I had a position in the middle of the boat, an ideal spot for shooting. Tom sat at the rear so he could handle the engineer's chores and also take care of the steering.

A seal is attracted by an unusual noise — we would create unusual noises by rubbing the butts of our rifles against the gunnels of the canoe. Soon, a bobbing head could be seen approaching. The seal would dive under the water and swim closer, then the bobbing head would again appear as the animal made a closer inspection of the source of the unfamiliar sound. Not until it reached approximately twenty feet did we consider it a suitable target. A dead seal would float for approximately one minute before it sank. During this minute it was necessary to start the outboard motor and maneuver the boat close enough to permit Albert's Boy to jab the animal with a harpoon.

The stories I read about Eskimos portrayed them throwing a harpoon with such deadly force and accuracy that it would pierce the animal's hide and insert the harpoon head firmly in its flesh. As I later learned, Albert's Boy was powerful. But when a slow-starting motor forced him to hurl his harpoon no further than ten feet it barely penetrated the seal's skin, and held only long enough to haul the animal into a position that allowed Tom to grab it by a flipper.

We piled our catch on the shore and covered it with rocks to provide the necessary protection against scavengers. The seals would still be good for food during the coming winter, providing sustenance for both man and dog.

Every seal hunt meant that the Crawfords would have fresh seal steaks for supper. They both ate them with relish but to me they tasted like tough leather fried in fish oil.

Upon my arrival at Repulse, drinking water was still available from the summer supply source. This consisted of a small pond filled above the drainage area of the post buildings. Within three weeks, however, the ice on the pond became too thick to be easily broken. It was time to obtain the winter's water supply. Using an ice saw, blocks were cut from the solid surface of the pond. Nature had been most generous —not only had she provided a fresh supply of frozen ice, she also provided a fresh supply of frozen snow. Thanks to the snow, the ice could be transported to the living quarters by dogsled. The two unbroken pups were not alone in their need to be introduced to the wonders and joys of arctic sledding. I also required a few lessons.

I received instructions on the proper way to grab a dog and render it helpless. This could be accomplished by pressing down on the animal's lower jaw. Once again, I was happy to be wearing my heavy duffle-lined mitts. Although pressing down on the dog's jaw renders it harmless, it also tests the sharpness of the canine's teeth. The dogs made no effort to conceal the fact that they would have preferred to continue their summer freedom. But the skill that Tom and Albert's Boy showed in catching and harnessing the team soon established who was in control. One of the pups took to working as a sleigh dog immediately. No amount of persuasion could induce the other to run and pull with the team. After making the trip for ice, both Tom and Albert's Boy were convinced it would never be a sleigh dog.

As soon as the dogs were harnessed they were driven the five hundred yards to the pond. Even though my efforts at dog harnessing had been somewhat of a failure, I felt certain I could excel at the next segment of the winter preparation chore. Albert's Boy had the appearance of being anything but a powerful man. He stood no more than five foot four and could weigh no more than one hundred and fifty pounds, even wearing his winter clothes. I took the ice tongs and squeezed them into the sides of a rectangular block of ice which weighed approximately two hundred pounds. I lifted it free from the water and slid it into position on the sled. I barely managed to refrain from giving a bow as I handed the tongs to the native. Albert's Boy took the tongs. He slid the second block of ice into place as easily as I had placed the first. Only one slight difference in our method of handling the tongs was evident — he used one hand while I used two. When the sleigh was finally loaded I found myself breathing heavily. The Inuit continued to breathe normally.

During some previous winter a platform had been built on the north side of the house by placing planks on top of empty gasoline drums. The multitude of free-running dogs almost certainly established a pollution level and this platform ensured that the ice would be stored well above it. Once the ice was stacked, it became the task of Old Peter the Fox Skinner to make certain that the topless gasoline drum behind the kitchen stove remained full of water. Every time I saw the elderly native carry a two-hundred-pound block of ice and hoist it over the edge of the barrel I received another reminder that I was living in a world where every man was all man.

At Repulse Bay summer ends quickly; autumn is brief; winter arrives early. Within five weeks of my arrival, not only did a good layer of snow cover the ground, but a couple of blizzards had blown it into drifts suitable for igloo building. The natives who resided in the post area lost no time in abandoning their skin tents and building snow houses. The deep drift that formed at the base of a hill, separating the Hudson's Bay Company buildings from the mission buildings, became a housing development overnight.

Each family originally built a large, one-roomed igloo. When drifting snow blocked their doorway, the residents dug themselves out by cutting blocks from the firmly packed snow. These blocks were used to fashion the walls and roof of a second room to the igloo. Since blizzards came frequently, the dwellings soon consisted of several rooms connected by tunnels.

If a family consisted of a father with married sons, each son and his family soon had separate rooms. One room might become a storage place for seal meat while another might be used to store the dog harness. Dogs were occasionally allowed to shelter in an entrance tunnel. With the coming of spring, the Inuit underwent a change of residence and moved from their multi-roomed igloos into one-roomed tents.

The white community consisted of the Crawfords, the Fathers from the mission, and myself. Long before my arrival at Repulse the social life pattern was well established. I found myself inserted into the slot reserved for the Hudson's Bay Company apprentice. Every Sunday night was bridge night with Tom and I forming a partnership against two of the Fathers. Only one slight deviation ever occurred in the fixed format of these card gatherings. We met at the mission one week and at the Hudson's Bay Company the next. Regardless of the closeness of the score, eleven thirty meant game over to allow sufficient time for a social snack before the Fathers celebrated their midnight mass.

Although two priests comprised the normal mission staff, a third missionary occasionally sat in as one of our bridge opponents at the beginning of the social season. His name was Father Henry or Attata Kaio (Father Red). His red beard automatically supplied the root for his Inuit name. The father had established a mission at Pelly Bay. His mission building consisted of a cave dug in the side of a hill. Lack of any other fuel meant that his only heat came from a seal-oil lamp. He had no facilities for cooking his food and a steady diet of frozen fish caused his stomach to relay objections too painful to be ignored. Consequently, he had spent a year in Montreal eating the type of food his digestive system was trained to accept.

Now, with a well-healed stomach, he impatiently waited for a dog team so he could return to Pelly Bay. In order to take the gospel to an area it would otherwise never have reached, this man was willing to forsake the basic comforts of life. When he outfitted himself for his trip back to Pelly Bay he remarked that he possessed neither dishes nor cutlery; at his mission he had no need for them.

The two resident priests at Repulse were a French Canadian and a younger chap who spoke Parisian French. Two years earlier, this young priest had fallen into the snow-covered breathing hole of a seal, while he was walking on the bay ice. Drowning usually resulted from this sort of accident. However, by discarding his solidly frozen mitts, he managed to claw his way from the frigid waters back onto the solid ice. During the hike back to the mission his hands became so badly frostbitten that amputation seemed almost certain to prevent gangrene from spreading to the balance of his body. But during his stay in a Montreal hospital, through some miracle, circulation returned to his fingers. His hands remained intact, but all the knuckles were enlarged and the finger flexibility was severely limited.

Transporting the ingredients for wine making proved to be both easier and more economical than transporting the finished product. Consequently, the Fathers made their own sacramental wine. Once the wine for altar use had been siphoned off, the residue in the bottom of the keg remained. Nothing is wasted in the Arctic. By again adding water to this sediment and letting whatever fermentation was still possible take place, a palatable drink for social purposes was produced. Unfortunately, the quantity of wine consumed at social functions far exceeded the quantity of wine consumed at the altar. Often we found ourselves drinking the product derived from the third re-run of the mash. This tasted as if rinse water, used to clean out the wine cask, had been bottled. But the watered-down liquid refreshments failed to dilute the conviviality of the gatherings.

When the Hudson's Bay Company post played host for the bridge sessions, homemade beer was served as the hospitality beverage. Tom made certain that the cargo of the *Fort Severn* contained a supply of malt and hops. Although many items were in short supply at Repulse Bay, spare time existed in abundance. Since we could set our own priorities, we gave brewing endeavors the necessary care and attention they warranted. Directions were followed explicitly. An extra filtering ensured a clear product. The taste of the bottled and matured beverage warranted the meticulous care exercised to produce it. For the first time in my life I found I enjoyed the taste of a glass of beer.

My liking for beer could in part be explained by my change in eating habits. Before arriving at Repulse, only the reluctance of offending my host prevented me from endeavoring to cut the fat off bacon and eat only the lean. Before leaving Repulse, I could cut a slice off a pound of lard and eat it like a youngster eats a chocolate bar. This change in eating habits showed. Prior to my craving for fats and other heat-producing foods I boasted a slim, trim, thirty-inch waist. My new eating habits added five inches to my waist and forty pounds to my weight.

Winter Travel

Tom had spent sufficient time in the arctic to know that long winters become even longer if one fails to become involved in some physical activity. He was also aware that two men could find irritating characteristics in each other if they spent the entire season continually in each other's company, no matter how compatible they were at the outset. Consequently, as soon as sufficient snow had fallen to make winter travel possible, he decided I should go on a deer-hunting and trap-setting trip.

Because of Tom's generous nature we were to be equal partners and split the catch on a fifty-fifty basis. He had the necessary gear, the dog team, and the know-how. I balanced his contributions with a large supply of eagerness to share in the profits.

A free loan of a butcher knife with an overdeveloped business end provided me with five per cent of the necessary gear. Although it had obviously been designed and manufactured with a different function in mind, this instrument was universally used as a snow knife throughout the eastern Arctic.

A ten-minute lecture on the techniques used in setting traps to catch the white fox provided me with ten per cent of the required know-how.

The white fox is a curious animal; anything different or changed in his domain warrants his immediate investigation. Whenever a trap is set, it is common practice to build a snow monument which serves a dual purpose. It not only attracts the fox, but also provides a marker for the trapper when he makes the next round of his traps. However, the animal's sense of smell often allows the bait to attract him long before the monument falls within his field of vision. Although I never witnessed it personally, I heard stories about how the Eskimos had their wives urinate at a trap site during their menstrual period. The stories claimed that these smell-baited traps were always successful. The natives did not coin the phrase "waste not want not," but they certainly lived by it.

The almost unending drifting snow caused by the almost unending wind would soon hamper or even prevent the action of a trap set on the snow's surface. To avoid this, a hole was cut in the windpacked snow that was the right size to house the trap. A block was cut slightly larger in diameter than the hole and placed, like a lid, over the set and baited trap. By skillful snow knife surgery this block was scraped until the outline of the trap became clearly visible. The trap was easily anchored by burying the end of the chain in snow, packing it firmly, adding moisture and allowing ten minutes for freezing.

Albert's Boy and his brother-in-law were assigned to teach me all the joys, trials, and tribulations of arctic travel. The features and the curly hair of the brother-in-law indicated he had a strain of Portuguese blood in his veins. Since none of the other natives had even a hint of a wave in their hair, we referred to the brother-in-law by the obvious name of "Curly."

For a course to be complete, a lecture portion should complement the practical workshop. Tom provided the lecture part of my course on arctic survival.

"Never venture out of sight from the others without carrying a snow knife," he said. "In the case of a blizzard it is always possible to make a windbreak out of snow blocks and walk back and forth behind it. Walking keeps you awake and your blood circulating. Lie down and you've taken the first step toward freezing to death. If you doze off hope for pleasant dreams. You have little hope of ever waking up."

Albert's Boy and Curly kept busy with various preparatory chores. Possibly because they considered it to be the most essential preparation, they began by icing the sled runners. Sufficient boiling water was added to a supply of fine black earth to form a mixture that was the right consistency for molding. This mixture was applied to the steel shoes of the wooden runners. The below-zero temperature soon froze the mud firmly to the metal. The komutik rested upside down on a couple of oil drums overnight. The next morning the natives used a long carpenter's plane on the molded mud shoes. They smoothed the shoes until they assured themselves that any bumps or hollows, which could impede easy sliding over the snow, were eliminated. Next they applied the final step. After taking a mouthful of water, they used their mouths as syringes to spray the frozen mud. As they sprayed, they wiped the resulting, rapidly forming layer of ice with a piece of polarbear hide. After several thin layers of ice were applied, the natives finally felt satisfied that an acceptable degree of slippery smoothness was reached. The sleigh was placed upright on the snow and given a performance test. One native stood about ten feet from each end, each giving the *komutik* light pushes with his feet to slide it back and forth. Since the Inuit refrained from any further icing, the runners had apparently reached an acceptable degree of slidability.

With my new deerskin parka, mukluks and moosehide mitts I considered my clothing adequate for taking an arctic journey. Tom, however, had different ideas. The sealskin mukluks were summer boots. *Kamiks,* or fur boots, comprised winter footwear. The *kamik* tops ended just above the wearer's ankles; the duffle stockings that completed the foot comfort package reached well above the knees. A pair of caribou-hide knee pants were correct dress for outdoor activities during the winter months. I received a second caribou-fur parka to replace my heavy woolen coat-sweater. In the native tongue this garment was referred to as an *artigee.* The Inuit also called the heavy woolen shirts we carried in the company store *artigees.* Due to the fact Tom practically lent me the shirt off his back, I now found myself properly outfitted for winter travel.

Since the fur on the caribou-hide *artigee* turned inward it functioned marvellously as a hair shirt. Underwear and a heavy doeskin shirt protected my skin from the shedding hair. The natives often wore their *artigees* without any protective garments under them, never giving any visible sign that the hair caused the slightest degree of irritation.

A Primus stove, a supply of gasoline, a steel thermos filled with steaming hot tea, three tin mugs and a boiling pot constituted the non-edible items in our grub box. Flour, lard, hardtack, jam, saccharine, salt and tea comprised the groceries usually carried. As an extra goodie for me, however, a supply of frozen lumps of bannock-dough biscuits was packed. Meat would be obtained enroute or the humans would share the dog's supply of frozen seal.

The natives each carried a rifle. I carried two — the twenty-two on loan from Mrs. Crawford and a thirty-thirty on loan from Tom.

Rather than the early departure I anticipated, we did not leave the post until mid-morning. Both the Crawfords were there to see me off. I noticed the families of the natives remained in their igloos. I later learned that the natives seldom bid each other farewell.

In the early autumn, whenever the sea is calm, the arctic cold causes ice to form. This ice lacks the strength to withstand the pressure and suction created by the rising and receding tides, consequently, it cracks and breaks into blocks. These blocks are washed ashore by the incoming tide resulting in an accumulation of jagged cakes along the shoreline.

By the time the winter cold forms ice strong enough to withstand the pressures of the rising and falling tide, this accumulation forms a barrier with peaks rising from ten to twenty feet. By chopping a pathway through this icy barrier, egress to the bay could be obtained. Albert's Boy and Curly took up positions on each end of the *komutik* and guided it through this pathway. Once we eased our way through the barrier, we reached a flat surface of snow-covered ice that stretched as far as the eye could see.

We all climbed aboard the sled and began skimming over the salt-sea ice at speeds from ten to fifteen miles per hour. My introduction to dog team travel in the Eskimo fashion confirmed the impression conveyed by the movies. Moreover, snowshoes were unnecessary since the lower mean temperature meant the drifts could easily carry the weight of a man on their surface.

This was dog team travelling at its finest. I tightened the drawstring on my parka hood. We were heading in a southwest direction and the day was perfectly calm. There was no doubt about it — any trip that began this way would be a fun trip all the way. Even the pup that considered life as a sled dog incompatible with his plans galloped beside the team, thoroughly enjoying himself.

In the typical fan-type hitch that was universally used by the Inuit, a single trace attached each of the ten dogs to the komutik. In the center of the draw bar a sealskin belt provided an easy method of securing the traces to the sleigh. An ivory bolt on one end of this belt turned crossways through a buttonhole in the other end and made a secure fastener. A ring carved from walrus tusk was fastened to the end of each trace. The drawbar belt passed through these rings and was then fastened.

The use of ivory in the harness was not a method of displaying wealth. In their day-to-day struggle for existence the natives used whatever material they had available and, whenever they managed to kill a walrus, ivory became available.

In theory, the fan-type hitch permitted the dogs to fan out as they pulled the sleigh. In practice, the lead dog was the only one that kept a constant position in relation to the rest of the pack. The remainder crossed from side to side constantly, entangling the traces so that the original six to eight feet of free length became so short that the dogs jostled each other as they ran. Albert's Boy took up a position near the forward end of the sleigh and braced his feet against the drawbar. Then he grasped the ten traces in his right hand and pulled the sled forward until the traces between his hand and the draw bar hung loose. He unfastened the clasp which secured them to the komutik. After removing his mitts, he somehow managed to untangle each individual trace without freeing any of the galloping dogs. Once the traces were untangled, the ivory ring on the end of each one was threaded with the drawbar belt, which in turn was secured with the ivory fastener.

Driving an Eskimo dog team constituted work for an active man. It required the continuous use of the Inuit whip. An Inuit whip has a three-foot handle and at least a twenty-foot lash. As soon as Albert's Boy laid his whip aside to untangle the traces, the dogs' pace would slacken. Curly immediately uncoiled his lash. I soon learned that he delighted in exercising his prowess with his dog-team accelerator. He would point to a spot on a loitering dog, crack his whip so that the tip of the lash ruffled the dog's fur at the exact spot he had designated. At the sudden forward surge of the dog he would laugh. Neither Albert's Boy or Curly found it necessary to let the dog feel the stinging bite of the lash; the constant warnings they gave by ruffling the dog's fur proved sufficient.

After travelling non-stop for a couple of hours we arrived in the middle of nowhere. The natives decided this would make an ideal lunch stop. Curly cut a couple of snow blocks and built a wind break while I placed the Primus stove in the shelter of this screen and lit it. Soon a pot full of virgin snow turned into boiling water and we dug into our supply of hardtack. The natives greased their hardtack generously with lard while I used mine to make strawberry jam sandwiches. We emptied the thermos of the scalding hot tea, threw a hand-measured quantity of tea leaves into the empty bottle, and filled it with boiling water. The natives threw a generous helping of tea leaves into the remainder of the boiling water. We carried a thermos large enough to fill each of the enamel mugs twice. For me this was more than sufficient, however my companions each consumed an additional two and a half mugs of the steaming beverage. Dishwashing consisted of wiping our snow knives in the snow and shaking the tea leaves from the mugs and boiling pot. Albert's Boy cracked his whip over the lead dog's head and once again we were on our way. The lunch hour lasted a full twenty minutes.

Two additional travel hours brought us to firm land on the southern side of Repulse Bay. The first four hours of my trip were an enjoyable experience. Travel was swift and the only physical effort required by me consisted of maintaining my balance on the loaded *komutik*. But hunting the arctic caribou and setting traps for the arctic fox provided the justification for making the trip. Both these animals exist on the arctic tundra and any further travel over the smooth bay ice would mean traveling without purpose. Although it took me all of five minutes to realize it, what started as a fun trip ended abruptly when we reached the southern shore of the bay — where the arduous part of the journey commenced.

I soon learned that overland travel by Inuit dog team differed greatly from the type of travel I had seen portrayed in the movies. Immediately we began to assist the dogs in pulling the sleigh up the numerous hills and hummocks that formed the foundation of the rocky terrain. The sleigh had to be manually braked on the downhill trips. Braking was accomplished by grasping one of the lines that lashed the load to the sled, keeping your knees locked, digging your heels into the snow and plowing two furrows with your feet until the gully at the bottom had been reached. If the covering of snow had been deep enough to form a soft plowing field free from obstacles, the downhill journey would have been fun. But boulders of all shapes, forms, and sizes jutted just above or lurked just below the surface of the snow. Almost every descent collected its toll in bruised feet and sprawling people. However, it finally provided me with an arctic activity in which I could excel. I definitely led my companions in the number of sprawls taken.

While we traveled over the frozen bay I had no difficulty keeping my directions straight. When traveling in view of a shoreline stretching in an east-west direction, it is easy. But once we started overland and I lost sight of the shore, I also lost all sense of direction. To me every hump and hollow looked exactly the same as the last. Although, as Tom explained, these gullies always sloped downhill to the sea, they do not do so in straight lines. After following the twisting bottom of the first gully for half an hour, I had no idea which way was which. In fact, after braking the sled on its downhill runs, I was beginning to feel that if I took many more spills, I would not even know which way was up. My guides, however, had landmarks that spelled out to them when and where to turn in order to continue traveling on a well-established route. They discussed the merits of each sign and, at times, Albert's Boy would take the trouble to explain to me in his understandable English that a certain heap of rocks made a marker. Although we were actually following a trail designated by native road signs, I had the sensation that we were wandering aimlessly. Meal times and rest times followed only the flexible schedule dictated by the natives' whims. Soon I found myself with only a vague idea of the time of day. By consulting my pocket watch and checking the position of the sun, it was possible to make an educated guess at the general direction. Unfortunately the traveling garb I wore did not provide watch pockets, and to reach my watch I had to partially disrobe. The temperature made it far more comfortable for me to remain fully clothed. I decided to place comfort ahead of accurate knowledge of direction and time. After all, until my native guides became lost, I had no cause for worry.

As we rounded one of the many hummocks, Albert's Boy pointed to the southern slope of a ridge. "Good place for trap," he said.

With meticulous care I followed Tom's instructions. Carefully I scooped out the right-sized hole, placed a bait in the bottom, set the trap and finally shaved a lid to paper thinness. We were still within a hundred yards of the set when the pup who had wholeheartedly rejected the chance of a career as a sleigh dog managed to unearth the bait and gobble it in one gulp without springing the trap. According to native philosophy, arctic survival meant everything and everybody served some useful function. Curly said something in Eskimo and laughed. "Him make good bait," Albert's Boy answered my questioning look as he pointed to the pup.

The Inuit never make statements purely in jest; they mean every word they utter. I withdrew Mrs. Crawford's twenty-two from its case and made certain the dog would be used for fox meat. The advice proved to be good — we caught three foxes using the dog-baited set.

It was the early part of the season and the mild part of winter. For this reason the boys did not consider building a full igloo necessary. They merely made walls of snow blocks and used additional hunks of snow as anchors to fasten a tent over the walls to form a roof. During the night the wind blew this roof off our shelter. The Inuit sprang from their sleeping bags, chased and caught the tent, and soon had it again secured in place.

I was still wearing all my clothes, with the exception of my outer parka and I watched the proceedings from the protection of my sleeping bag. I felt chilled and could see nothing pleasant in the situation. The natives were sweating and laughing. Moreover, except for their *kamiks,* they were stark naked. Laughter seemed to be the only expression of emotion the Inuit used. I remember one chap telling how his brother fell through a seal's breathing hole in the salt-sea ice and drowned. He laughed all the time he was relaying the misadventure.

In the morning not a dog could be found. The thirty- to forty-mile-per-hour wind had drifted snow until they were completely covered. The Eskimos jabbed a length of steel rod into any likely looking mound and were soon rewarded by a few yelps and the emergence of the ten dogs.

The following night, in the hope it would provide a full night of uninterrupted sleep, the boys decided to stop early enough to build a full igloo. Again, the length of steel was used. This time it functioned as a test rod to locate an acceptable pocket of snow. In order to build a decent igloo the snow should be a single layer firmly packed to a depth of about three feet. Blocks cut from layered snow have a tendency to split at the seams. When he had located a suitable snow patch, Albert's Boy extended his arms. He used one arm as a pivot, the other as a marker and drew a circle in the snow's surface. Then he took his snow knife and began to cut blocks from the inner circumference of the circle. These blocks were placed so that they formed a wall around the rim of the circle from where they had been cut. While Albert's Boy continued to cut blocks and hoist them into place, Curly carved the first three so that they began an upward spiral from the snow's surface. He then made certain that all blocks fitted snugly together by pushing them against each other and deftly slashing the join with his snow knife.

As Albert's Boy continued to position them on the wall Curly continued to carve an upward spiral. At times he helped his companion hoist a block into position. While both natives worked from the inside, I became the outside man at the snow house. I was handed a wooden, paddle-like shovel with a sufficient handle for one-handed use, and given the task of throwing powdered snow over the portion of the structure that had been completed.

Albert's Boy continued to cut a layer of blocks from the circle until one circular block remained. He placed this to one side. He now divided the floor of the structure into two arcs. The larger of these took up two thirds of the floor area and this formed the sleeping bench portion of our shelter. From the smaller arc sufficient blocks were cut to finish the igloo. This space was reserved for the Primus stove, the grub box and any other material that had to be stored away from the bite of the hungry dogs.

Curly cut his way out of the igloo. Taking the circular block his fellow native had placed to one side he climbed to the top of the snow house. He used the block to fill the small remaining section of open roof. The long blade of Albert Boy's snow knife could be seen describing circles in the air as it simultaneously trimmed both the edge of the block and the edge of the hole. This induced the former to fit snugly into the latter. The house now stood fully completed and ready for occupancy. I was informed this had been a hurried construction job; the project had taken thirty-five minutes. An igloo built for a winter's occupancy usually took a couple of hours to construct.

While the natives performed a few other necessary camp chores, such as feeding the dogs, I crawled inside and lit the Primus stove. After I made tea and fried bannock, I began to feel comfortable for the first time in seventy-two hours. The stories I read as a boy were true —igloos were warm. Curly entered and became quite excited. I'd managed to heat the snow house above freezing point and it was melting. He summoned his brother-in-law who explained to me, "You burn 'em up house."

No sooner had we finished supper than Curly said something in his native tongue and laughed. Albert's Boy joined him in the display of merriment. Then he turned to me: "He say everybody smoke like hell. He gotta shit."

We all built fat cigarettes from my tobacco. While we were puffing furiously on these cancer sticks Curly picked up his snow knife. He began by making a good-sized air hole in the roof of our shelter. Then he rolled his polar-bear-hide ground sheet to one side, dug a hole in the snow bench and performed the necessary function. He quickly replaced the block of snow he had removed to make the indoor toilet and rolled the bearskin back into place. Even though the small confines of the igloo had been filled with tobacco smoke, the stench proved almost unbearable for the next few minutes. The roof vent proved to be an absolute must.

Curly's action did not in any way reflect a lack of consideration for either Albert's Boy or myself. Outside, ten untethered dogs roamed at will. To attempt his elimination function beyond the security that the wall provided would have meant being ripped limb from limb by a pack of hungry huskies.

We were now in deer country. Traveling stopped frequently while one of the natives took a telescope and climbed to the top of the highest hill to scan the countryside for a glimpse of the arctic caribou. They always returned sadly shaking their heads.

Deer were scarce that year. We had left the post with a good two weeks' supply of food. After three weeks there was very little of it left. Curly, however, loved to fish. Often before breaking camp, Albert's Boy would take a rifle and spend the morning on foot searching for deer. Curly would chop a hole in the ice of the nearest pond and stand for hours, jigging a lure in the open water that the hole exposed, hoping to coax a fish within striking distance of his gaff. His lure consisted of a home-made fly, carved entirely from ivory in the shape of a miniature fish. As the Eskimo jigged it up and down, two moving fins gave it the appearance of being a swimming object. The gaff resembled King Neptune's trident. The center tine had been fashioned from a length of metal rod. Using a piece of broken file, Curly sharpened the tine to the ultimate. The outer tongs were fashioned from ivory and lashed to the wooden shaft with sealskin thong. Their ends hooked inwards and upwards to allow them to spring out and over whatever game was speared. Their design ensured the game remained on the spear until the native decided it should be released. Curly's fishing efforts varied from good to extremely successful. Never did he return empty-handed. This allowed us to continue eating the choicest Arctic char, but I still have no desire to feast on a fish dinner.

One day close to the trail the Eskimos were following, two ptarmigan stood huddled on the sunny side of a rock. I took the twenty-two from its case and, while the natives continued along the trail, made certain we had fowl for a change of diet. The following morning both natives set out to hunt deer on foot while I remained in the igloo to cook and dress the birds. By the time my companions returned, the ptarmigan were well stewed. Suddenly, after we had started eating, I mentioned that I had forgotten to remove the crops during the cleaning process. Albert's Boy immediately grabbed one and Curly took the other, devouring them as if they were a real delicacy. Tom later explained to me that the greenery in a bird's crop made a salad bowl for the natives.

Whenever men go deer hunting, part of the pleasure of the hunt is sitting around the campfire at night and swapping yarns. We didn't have a campfire, but a snow bench provided a good place to sit around. In our group Albert's Boy excelled at story telling. Of course he had an advantage. His experience as a sailor allowed him to yarn about both cultures in both tongues. He told us about riding in a hotel elevator. His description was vivid: "Igloo go down. My stomach go up." To add emphasis to the fact that his stomach went up, he gave an excellent imitation of regurgitation.

He described the frustrations he encountered when he went for a stroll along the Montreal streets: "All big igloos look alike. No stones to mark trail. Me lose 'em."

But his bathroom experiences proved to be the highlight of his adventures: "Me take off clothes. Me take big brush. Me scrub 'em all over." As he spoke he pantomimed his use of the brush across his back and over his stomach.

Although Curly had doubtless heard this story before, his face took on an incredulous expression. Washing one's body all over was too much for an Inuit to believe. Even though Albert's Boy had me vouch for his story, Curly remained skeptical. To him it didn't make sense to bathe in an igloo. A stone house like Albert's Boy's description of the hotel was colder than a snow house. And the temperature had to be kept below freezing in a snow house.

Another of his brother-in-law's stories that Curly found difficult to believe was the one about an igloo that moved: "We sit. No *koolitah*.

No *artigee*. Outside cold. We warm. We go next igloo and eat. Night we sleep. And igloo no stop. Go like thirty dogs pull *komutik*."

I had no knowledge of the amount of dog power required to equal one horsepower. Nor did I know the horsepower rating or speed of the locomotive pulling the train that transported Albert's Boy and his fellow Inuit crew members from Montreal to the lumber camp. But even if I had this information at my fingertips and fluency in the Eskimo tongue, I would have been unable to explain why the estimate of thirty dogs was slightly on the conservative side. The native vocabulary did not contain the necessary words.

After a good three weeks of traveling, the natives decided to make one final effort to locate some deer. Instead of breaking camp one morning, they left me with the bedrolls and other excess traveling baggage, setting out with the empty sleigh and their rifles. They returned after six hours. One glance at their walk and the gleam in their eyes was all I required to realize their last desperate attempt was successful. They managed to get within rifle range of a pair of deer. The doe was felled, but the buck had taken to his heels and disappeared. The natives left the female where she fell. In the morning, Albert's Boy explained, we would return and possibly the buck would be beside his dead mate.

The next morning proved this reasoning was correct. When we approached the scene of the previous day's success, we were greeted by the somewhat pathetic sight of an animal waiting for its dead mate to revive. The natives brought the dogs to a halt. They threw out their sled anchor (a two-pronged hook attached to the sleigh with a length of sealskin thong) and taking a rifle each, set off on foot to shoot the remaining deer. When they were within range they both fired and missed. The animal began to run. The dogs strained at their traces until they pulled the sled anchor loose. I found myself riding on a bouncing sleigh with bullets from the natives' rifles whistling around my ears. I withdrew Tom's thirty-thirty from its case and aimed at the fleeing deer. Somehow the bounce of the sled and the jump of the deer were synchronized and I hit it on my first shot. The natives could not conceal their amazement. Possibly because my own amazement reduced me to a state of shock, little excitement was reflected in my face. My deadpan expression conveyed the impression that shooting a running caribou from a bouncing sled constituted such a simple feat for me that I could accomplish it any time such conditions prevailed. This one lucky hit proved sufficient to establish a reputation among the natives that *Teegeeractee* was a crack rifle shot.

Immediately, the natives skinned the warm animal. The other, which had frozen stiff, they lashed to the sleigh. When we arrived back at the post an effort would be made to salvage its hide.

Two deer did not justify all the time we spent hunting. However, all our traps were set, our hardtack was eaten and our supply of gasoline for the Primus stove was almost exhausted. Albert's Boy explained that since I had a whiteman's stomach and could not survive long on Inuit food we would return to the post. I explained that there was no need to travel home on my account. I must have used words the native failed to understand because my argument to continue the hunt went unheeded.

Four days later we arrived back at Repulse Bay. I was tired and hungry, but my greatest discomfort was my beard. It was dirty and had a tendency to curl back into my skin which produced a continuous itch. Before I removed my duffle socks I removed my facial foliage, making a mental note to take shaving equipment on any future trips.

The Dark Days

I was taught that winter nights in the arctic lasted for six months. I now found this teaching to be incorrect. The winter nights at Repulse never extended beyond twenty-two hours. During the period between mid-November and late January, a couple of twilight hours substituted for the morning, mid-day, afternoon and evening daylight. A person could see well enough in this dusk to feed more fuel to the fires and perform a few other manual chores. But the majority of tasks, especially those embodying reading or writing, could only be performed with the assistance of artificial light.

Throughout this cycle of limited daylight, life continues —but it does not continue as normal. Lack of sunlight produces a lethargy in people and tends to change the compatible to the incompatible. Tom was aware of only one method to lessen, if not prevent, the friction that would inevitably build up between two white men during this period of extended nights. He never studied the section of psychology that explains how strenuous physical activity bleeds off excess emotion. Consequently, he spoke from experience as he expressed himself in a straight forward manner: "We've both got to get up and keep going."

No radio station gave a weather report for the Repulse Bay However, during the winter I found any forecast absolutely unnecessary. Upon awakening I would lie in bed and listen. If I could hear the wind howling outside I knew a blizzard was in progress; if I could not hear the wind I knew a blizzard was on the way.

To ensure that we had an activity of sufficient interest to occupy us during the calm days we established two trap lines. One of these extended west from the post and the other extended east. A six-hour walk was required to cover either line. During the winter we decided to extend the line to the east so that a three-day trip by dog team was necessary to cover the entire route. This extension was created primarily to avoid the friction that continuous companionship produces. One of us could make the trip while the other remained at the post; any extra pelts we obtained would be a fringe benefit.

Albert's Boy agreed to be our third partner on the trap-line extension. He and I left the post one calm, clear moonlit morning to select the most promising spots and set the traps. All went well until the following day. When I woke up I could not hear any wind, the igloo felt extremely warm and not a speck of light penetrated the roof of our shelter. Suddenly my companion's voice interrupted the absolute tranquility. "We in snowbank," he said.

I rolled over to return to sleep but it was not to be. I felt myself being shaken while the words, "We in snow bank," were repeated continually.

Perhaps because my return to physical activeness proved to be too slow for the native's liking he changed his tactics. He stopped speaking and I could feel the snow falling on my face. I stared at the ceiling, endeavoring to see a shaft of light through the roof vent. But my semi-awake senses only registered snow continually falling on my face. Slowly I became aware of the vague outline of a moving figure. As my night vision improved, a sense of awareness penetrated my mind. I realized that the moving figure was Albert's Boy standing on a block and cutting at the roof. Suddenly, a gush of fresh air indicated he had succeeded in creating a full-sized opening.

I struck a match and lit the Primus stove. I held my watch close to its light and realized we had overslept. It was ten thirty. My watch had not yet run down and the beginning of the mid-day dusk eased through the opening.

Snow had also fallen on the native's body. This had melted and turned into icy water. However, the Inuit seemed to be unaware of any discomfort as he dressed without first drying himself.

"Now we look," he said. "Maybe go home, maybe stay here."

Before we could look we had to dig ourselves out of the igloo. Albert's Boy immediately began to cut blocks from the snow to make a new egress. These he handed to me to stack inside our shelter. Soon he had a stairway that led to the top of the snowdrift. I began to convert a kettle full of the clean snow into boiling water. The blocks that were not required for this cooking chore, were pushed into the stairway and then piled on top of the drift.

Albert's Boy studied the white landscape. "Go home," he said.

"Tea first, then go," I replied.

I took a look at the weather. The storm appeared to be abating. But in any event, the homeward journey could be accomplished since the wind would be at our backs. Any attempt to travel in another direction would have been a foolhardy venture with an extremely limited chance of survival. This might be an excellent area for setting fox traps but there would be better days to do the setting.

As we were into the season with the longest nights and the shortest days we did not linger over a leisurely breakfast. Already, the twilight began to recede. We wanted to be on our way before the darkness of the blizzard totally enveloped us. Once harnessed, the dogs could easily be persuaded to return to the post, regardless of the visibility. They would be running with the wind and on their way home.

What I had thought was an abating blizzard proved to be merely a short lull in a vicious storm. The wind began to increase in velocity and I began to experience my first real taste of arctic cold. I can only estimate the wind chill factor. However, the wind velocity seemed to vary between forty and sixty miles per hour and Tom later told me that the post thermometer read minus fifty-eight degrees Fahrenheit. The twin caribou parkas, reinforced by my heavy underwear, shirt and sweater, were insufficient in withstanding this weather. Cold penetrated and stabbed at my back as if needles of ice were driven right through my garments.

We didn't make the usual stops for tea. This meant that Albert's Boy also felt the biting cold. Normally, he never failed to stop for a mug-up at my expense as frequently as he could justify the stops.

Still, even without the frequent tea stops I felt the need to pass my water. The fur pants I wore were tailored with comfort from the wind and cold in mind, and conveniences for toilet functions had been ignored. Although my hands were chilled in the process, undressing posed no problem. Once I returned my hands to the comfort of my moosehide mitts the chill soon disappeared. My problems started when I tried to dress again. Immediately, when I removed my hands from my mitts, my fingers became too stiff to function. Finally Albert's Boy came to my rescue and dressed me as if I were an infant who had not yet mastered the art of fastening buttons or tying strings. The Inuit only wore unlined sealskin mitts, yet his fingers remained supple enough to roll a cigarette from my tobacco as soon as he had finished his nursemaid chores.

Although it was well past midnight, visibility was nil and we were not due back at the post for two days, a reception committee of Tom and Curly met us at the beach. The dogs were cared for, the sleigh unloaded and all other homecoming chores accomplished — but I do not know how. I stumbled into the house and concentrated on absorbing as much heat as possible. I soon discovered that the penetrating cold I had felt stabbing my back was real; my back was frostbitten.

The Inuit are nomads. Occasionally a small tribe of traveling families would visit the post. At other times, if they wished to avoid the congestion created by large groups, a single family would arrive to trade.

Omik and his wife were one such family. Although they had been married for several years they still remained childless. To compensate for this oversight of nature, Mrs. Omik carried a doll in the baby pouch fashioned in the hood of her parka. She gave this plaything the attention and loving care that she would have given a real, live infant.

Like other mothers who would place their stark-naked babies on the warm kitchen floor to play, this lifeless toy was placed in a crawling position on the freshly scrubbed linoleum. She would regularly hold the doll in the approved position that allows a baby to make its toilet, then follow through by wiping its buttocks with her forefinger. Perhaps in an igloo she would have wiped her finger in the snow to clean it. But apparently she did not consider this cleansing operation possible in the kitchen.

An empty room off the kitchen was referred to as The Eskimo Room. The Omiks asked for and received permission to sleep in this room. Although natives rarely make an early departure, they had vacated the premises before we were up. Both had gone to the toilet before leaving. I know, because I had the task of cleaning up two heaps of excretion before the room could again be used. Fortunately, they made no attempt to first cut a sanitation hole in the floor.

Two weeks and three minor storms after my return from the aborted trap-setting expedition, the wind whipped up another blizzard. It made us wonder about the wisdom of having our stockpile of fuel so far from the house. It rendered indoor toilet facilities a must and accomplished several other nasty little things that arctic blizzards complete to perfection.

For example, at the height of the storm we received an unnecessary reminder that mechanical devices fail. The windcharger stopped charging. Although the hydrometer indicated that all the battery cells were fully charged, without constant recharging they would not remain that way. We couldn't phone for a repair man; we couldn't order another charger and expect delivery in less than nine months. That left us with two alternatives. We could repair the charger ourselves or forget the radios. I donned my warmest clothes and climbed the twelve-foot tower. I separated the malfunctioning machine from its base and quickly carried it to the center of the warm living room. Now, while the raging storm made outdoor activity almost impossible, we could occupy ourselves with an indoor task. Immediately the windvane, the propeller and many other pieces of the super-structure were stored in The Eskimo Room.

Before I ventured outside to bring the ailing machine into the comfort of our improvised workshop, Tom suggested that the carbon brushes needed replacing. A quick inspection of the generator proved his analysis to be correct. There were no spare brushes on hand at Repulse Bay. The earliest possible delivery date was late August, encompassing portions of four seasons and extending over half a year into the future.

Tom suggested an alternative to the long wait. He knew a spot on the west side of the store building where the British Canadian Arctic

Expedition had discarded several worn-out dry cells. Now he donned his outdoor clothing and ventured forth, taking a scoop shovel. Within ten minutes he returned carrying three one-and-one-half-volt batteries. Fortunately the natives had not discovered a use for worn-out dry cells.

We spread some old wrapping paper on the floor and began operating on a battery. With the aid of a chisel and a screwdriver we soon removed the center carbon post. The remainder of the battery immediately went into the firebox of the living room heater. We had pulled one over the natives. They had not yet discovered that worn-out batteries could be used for fuel.

A hacksaw, a file and a small supply of muscle power soon saw two brushes produced from the length of carbon. We both realized that the hardness of the carbon in the original equipment differed greatly from that in the replacements we had just fashioned. If this variation in hardness shortened the length of time the brushes would function effectively, then changing brushes would have to be added to our list of regular chores. We decided to store the balance of the discarded cells in the security of the warehouse. Hopefully, the stored batteries would ensure a supply of carbon sufficient enough to meet our needs until ship unloading time. We were, however, pleasantly surprised when only one more set of home-made brushes had to be carved before the supply vessel arrived.

Fortunately, not all the arctic storms caused outdoor damage that required repairs. However, the high velocity of the wind during a blizzard in the later stages of winter blew the radio antennae free from its mast, separating the lead-in wire from the aerial. The frequency on which we were permitted to operate required that the lead-in wire be attached at an exact distance from the end of the fixed-length antennae. It appeared we had a problem.

A copy of a text on typing together with a copy of *The Radio Operator's Handbook For 1939* formed our technical library. The handbook contained a formula to calculate not only the antennae length, but the correct location at which each branch of the two wire lead-ins should be attached. I calculated all the measurements twice, then slid the calculations under the radio. The next day I repeated the process and compared the results. Both sets of figures agreed.

When the wind finally subsided to a stiff breeze I donned my outdoor garb, opened the front door, and dug out the front steps. I climbed over the freshly drifted snow and located the antennae end still attached to the house. By tugging and digging I managed to free the length of wire from its covering of several feet of snow. My careful calculations had not been necessary. The solder marks from the original lead-in connections were still visible. We twisted and soldered the separated sections back together. Using a ladder we attached the antennae end back to the mast and tested our efforts. Communication with the outside world was again possible.

Although daylight varied between no-intensity to low-intensity, on calm nights the moon often provided fair visibility. Tom and I took advantage of these bright periods to cover one of our short trap lines. We painted the front sights of the twenty-two rifles with phosphorous, and as a result we were able to enjoy the fresh meat from arctic hare. In addition to the rifles, we each carried a snow knife. Even though we had no intention of becoming separated, Tom's arctic experience had taught him that it is safer to travel without a parka than without a snowknife, especially during the winter.

By scheduling our daytime activities to take advantage of the best available light, we frequently turned night into day. The once or twice per month trading activities negated most of the difficulties usually experienced by those who wander all night and cat nap all day.

Contact with the Wager Inlet outpost was initiated from Repulse Bay. And if contact was not entirely mandatory, it was definitely advisable, usually requiring dog team travel for a personal visit. Tom decided to make the first trip. The trap line that was established during the deer hunt followed the well-marked winter trail to Wager Inlet. Like other wage-paying organizations, the Hudson's Bay Company felt it had every right to make some demands on the time of the personnel to whom it was paying the wages. Consequently, neither Tom nor myself had been able to visit the traps since they were first set. This had not left the line neglected because Albert's Boy inspected it regularly. However, the Wager Inlet trip would allow Tom to become actively involved in that section of our trap line partnership.

There existed the slightest chance that Tom's absence might force me, with my limited knowledge of the Inuit tongue, to attempt to trade with a native. However, no language barrier problems were anticipated. The value for foxes would be established in the kitchen and Mrs. Crawford could be called on, if necessary, to interpret.

The day after Tom left I learned that high odds can sometimes cause erroneous predictions. A native arrived with foxes to trade. As anticipated, due to Mrs. Crawford's assistance, I encountered no problem in establishing the trade value of the foxes. I unlocked the store to allow the natives to do their window shopping.

By using heat produced from friction to ignite some highly combustible material, the natives eliminated their need to carry matches. And life in an igloo means complete freedom from the hazards of house fires. Even though an ember from the burning wick of a seal-oil lamp would occasionally fall on the floor, half-cooled embers did not set floors fashioned from well-packed snow on fire. Consequently, the Inuit were not too concerned about the need to be cautious when carrying a flame. For good reason Tom had warned me never to provide an Eskimo with a lantern when he wished to browse through the store. I lent them one of the flashlights that were reserved for the purpose.

Normally, trading proceeded at a brisk pace until the credit for the last half fox remained to be spent. But when the sticks representing four full foxes and one half fox remained to be bartered, the native and his family began to pick and choose with great care. How much tobacco would four sticks buy? How much chewing gum? Should they get another box of twenty-two shells or a second cigarette holder for the wife? Suddenly he came to a decision that caused a great deal of laughter among the family. The native decided that a watch would be his next purchase. Since the Inuit never referred to a timepiece to determine if it was mealtime, daytime or nighttime I had often wondered why several Big Ben pocket watches hung on the store wall beside the tobacco shelf. Now I knew. They were items for the native trade. I carefully removed one from the nail that was holding it in place and put it on the counter, removing three dollars worth of sticks. Trading stopped while the native wound the timepiece, pointed to the revolving second hand and then put it to his ear.

Finally we reached the point where four full foxes remained. Then it became obvious that these had been saved to purchase something special. But no matter how hard the native tried to describe the article, I could not understand either his words or his gestures. Finally I motioned for him to place the article he wished on the counter. He disappeared into the warehouse and emerged carrying two twenty-foot lengths of plank. Although the lumber did not have a price tag attached, I remembered a similar transaction that had taken place shortly after I arrived. By referring to my counter notes I found that these planks sold for ten dollars each. I removed the necessary two foxes worth of sticks from the pile. The Eskimo shook his head. I was positive it took one fox to buy one plank and there was no way I intended to cut the price. I motioned for him to replace the plank and I would replace the sticks. Again, he shook his head and this time he followed through by pushing the remaining sticks from the unspent heap to the pile that had been spent. It left me bewildered. In desperation we returned to the house. Mrs. Crawford explained that if my price was right the native could use up his credit on a later visit. Now, he wanted a new *komutik* and would pay two foxes for each runner. A final decision on the price could wait until the manager returned.

When the understanding was finally relayed to me, the natives resumed their tea party. Although the first gathering had exhausted the hardtack, plenty of tea remained. I retreated to the living room to enter the transactions in the official books. But I had scarcely started when excited laughter from the group of natives caused me to return to the kitchen. The watch had been completely dismantled. Wheels, springs and an assortment of bits and pieces lay scattered over the kitchen table. Half an hour later it was re-assembled and ran as perfectly as the day it left the factory. The Inuit's only tool consisted of the blade of a pocket knife.

A week before Tom arrived home from Wager Inlet the native ended his visit to Repulse Bay. Obviously he didn't anticipate any refund from an adjustment in the price he had paid for a pair of planks.

The confusion over the planks was easily explained. The set of sled runners previously sold were second hand and consequently they were reduced to half price. New *komutiks* to the natives were like new autos to the white man. Every Inuit who had seen the plank asked Tom the price. Although I must have heard two foxes per plank quoted a dozen times, when you don't speak the language you don't pick up details of the conversation.

A ton of coal landed at Repulse Bay cost one hundred dollars for freight. Consequently, the difference in cost between the best coal on the market and the poorest was marginal. Our supply of fuel consisted of the finest coal the Welsh mines could produce. The kitchen range and a heater in the living room supplied the heat for the house. In the interests of preserving fuel, we allowed the fire in the kitchen range to burn out during the night. In the interests of preserving all-night comfort we banked the fire in the heater.

One morning I woke up with a terrific headache. My entire consciousness was aware only of a head that throbbed with every beat of my heart. I felt the presence of intense cold and realized that someone had opened all the doors and let the frigid arctic air rush into every corner of the usually well-heated living quarters. Normally Tom, who rose first, would turn on the radio and let the sound of the morning news awaken me. This morning, instead of the somber tones of the announcer's voice, the laughter of Peter the Fox Skinner began to penetrate my semi-conscious mind. I slowly pulled on my clothes. With a somewhat drunken stagger I found my way into the living room to find a suffocating odor had enveloped the entire house. Tom had already dressed in his outdoor clothes and looked as seedy as I felt.

During the night snow had drifted over the chimney and cut off the air flow through the coal, causing the house to fill with manufactured gas. The fact that Peter arrived at ten o'clock for his mug of tea saved our lives. Usually we were up and about at seven. This morning the Eskimo, finding nobody around, wandered into the Crawfords' bedroom and managed to shake Tom into consciousness.

Tom and I cleaned the snow from the chimney, dismantled the stove pipes, took them outside and cleaned them of soot. After making certain everything was in order, we relit the fire. Now, rather than a poisonous gas-producing plant, we again had a warmth-producing heater.

Mrs. Crawford had taken her baby and gone to visit in an igloo. On Tom's suggestion we elected to make a trip around one of our back yard traplines.

Neither of us gave any thought to having breakfast or for that matter, lunch. The terrific pounding in my head lasted for a good three hours and I remained sick to my stomach for at least six. That evening when we returned from our hike, we both managed a small snack, but neither of us had the appetite usually generated from a walk around a trapline.

Around the end of January the gloom that had encompassed us all for the past two months began to lift. The twilight hours were replaced by sunlight. The sight of the sun gave everyone, including the post natives, an enormous lift in spirits. The tendency to snarl began to ease and occasionally we could manage an unforced smile. Winter confinement had ended.

Wager Inlet

We considered the radio to be an extremely efficient communication medium since it kept us informed of all the important happenings along the coast. But, whenever the happening was important to the natives, our system proved to be quite inferior to the *mukluk* telegraph. Consequently, we knew a mounted policeman was preparing to make a patrol from Chesterfield Inlet to Repulse Bay long before we received the radio message that he had left.

This meant I would have an opportunity to mail letters in which I could write those confidential phrases I felt too timid to broadcast to the rest of the world. I made prints of the most interesting snap shots I had taken and had five letters ready to mail.

But a day after leaving Wager Inlet, a native informed us that the policeman and his Inuit teamster had ended their journey. Eight days later a radio message confirmed the abrupt end to my dream of dispatching private mail. Advance warnings that the salt-sea ice could disintegrate at any time had influenced the police patrol to place caution ahead of adventure. They established a new destination to mark their journey's end, left the mail, and commenced their homeward trek.

Tumuk, the native who told us of the mountie's decision to cut short his patrol, volunteered his services, his sleigh and his dog team for a reasonable fee, to make the mail run. The mail had been left only six days' travel from Repulse Bay. It was decided that I would accompany the native. He spoke no English and I had an extremely limited vocabulary in his tongue. But since we intended to travel and let the dogs take care of the yapping, the language barrier caused little concern.

It was late in April. The company's business year ended on the thirtieth. A stock count had to be made of the trade goods and fur on hand at Wager Inlet. Tom decided it would be good experience for me to continue the trip to the outpost. I welcomed the idea of having a definite stopover that would break the monotony of traveling. A bit of counting and note-taking within the protection of a frame-constructed store building would certainly not be too exhorbitant a price to pay for this respite. Moreover, our supply of tobacco would last no more than another week. We anticipated that this limited supply could be sufficiently augmented by the Wager Inlet stock to prevent both Tom and myself from suffering withdrawal pains.

Once our itinerary had been firmly established and the financial arrangements completed, Tumuk lost no time in making his necessary preparations. His sled runners had to be iced with the thick coating necessary for mild weather. Instead of pouring a thin coating of warm water over the smooth mud, the native used a mixture of snow and water to make certain that the mud did not melt.

The local natives spent a good part of their time hunting seal on the salt sea ice. They observed no telltale cracks warning of an early breakup. Our route was planned to take advantage of the excellent sled causeway that the ice provided. We intended to cross the bay and follow the shoreline to its mouth. From there we would follow the coast to the mouth of Wager Inlet. There, the north shore of the inlet would serve as a guide to the mail cache and finally to the post itself. It would be smooth, easy traveling all the way. I would be able to sit on the *komutik,* remember the past, daydream of the future and ignore the miseries of the present.

The trip began exactly as I anticipated it would. Tumuk's whip-handling abilities rivaled those of Albert's Boy and Curly. While I lost myself in my daydreams of the future the native enjoyed every minute of the present. He shouted at his dogs, cracked his whip when necessary and periodically looked at me and grinned his pleasure. Occasionally he would look at the shoreline. Whenever the jagged ice permitted a clear view he would nod as if greeting some familiar rock formation. Although I'm certain he knew the shoreline well enough to have a nodding acquaintance with every rock along the way, the nod was his method of assuring me that we were making excellent time. Within six hours we began to travel through Roes Welcome Sound.

Suddenly the native's silence brought me back to the present. No longer did he amuse himself by cracking his whip and shouting at his dogs. He kept looking back, looking at me and looking at the shore. Something was wrong, very wrong, but I could not determine what. We had no common tongue by which to converse and Tumuk's emotional state had risen to such a degree that communication by sign language was impossible. To me everything appeared normal. I could not detect even the slightest clue of the misfortune that caused the Inuit's concern. After he drove the dogs closer to the shore, I saw the reason for his alarm. A gap of water, varying in width from fifteen to twenty feet, separated the continent of ice we were traveling on from the bulwark of jagged ice, rendering the shoreline unpenetrable.

I had heard stories of natives meeting an untimely end by drifting out to sea on ice floes. Since they usually treated the forces of nature with great respect, I wondered why they would abandon their usual caution and recklessly go sailing on a cake of ice. But I visualized little danger in our present position. We were on a cake of ice that stretched, without a break, for miles in each direction before finally fading into the horizon. I thought that the incoming tide would soon force our continent of ice against the continent of North America, eliminate the icy moat that now separated us and once more we would enjoy smooth sledding. If I had been more aware of the gravity of the situation my nonchalance would have been non-existent. The seas of unbroken ice soon crack and crumble into smaller cakes. These cakes bump and grind together, continually reducing their size; the surviving cakes float southward until they reach warmer water and eventually melt. My ignorance of this resulted in my complete lack of fear.

Tumuk kept close watch on the shore and closer watch on the water barrier as he drove on. Suddenly his diligent searching bore fruit. A level spot appeared in the wall of rough shore ice. He changed course and drove his team a good two hundred yards towards the center of the bay. He aimed the dogs directly at the open space on the shore and whipped, shouted and urged them forward at ice-melting speed. When they reached the water they were traveling too fast to even hesitate. The lead dog leaped. Her feet clutched at the icy bank. Tumuk's whip kept the team moving forward and almost immediately the dogs began scrambling from the icy water to the beach of solid, snow-covered terrain. We rode on the sleigh. Its eighteen-foot length, combined with our traveling speed, made it possible to bridge the gap without wetting the bottom of the load. We traveled a good mile inland before Tumuk permitted the dogs to slacken their pace.

Tumuk eventually allowed his panting team to stop, providing me with the opportunity to survey the surrounding area. We appeared to be traveling on the leveled top of an enormous pile of rocks, boulders and stones. Tumuk grabbed the sealhide case that contained his personal belongings and ran behind a boulder. In about ten minutes he returned somewhat embarrassed. He had changed his trousers. From the smell of the pair he now carried I had no difficulty determining the reason he had decided to change.

I made tea. Tumuk soon recovered from his recent fit of terror but he wanted no more harrying experiences with floating ice. He made me understand that we would abandon the coastal route and travel overland. I was far from overjoyed with this change of route since I had vivid memories of overland travel in the native manner. Still the letters I expected to pick up at the mail cache would be well worth the arduous journey to reach them. Also, a supply of nicotine to continue feeding my addicted body would be a worthwhile fringe benefit.

The natives gauge the length of a trip by the number of times they make camp before completing it. Tumuk pushed on for another four hours before stopping. Possibly he hoped to complete the trip in the same number of days the coastal route would have taken. To accomplish this it would be necessary to increase the number of hours of travel time per day. Since this would in no way be stretching his endurance, it never occurred to him that he might be stretching mine. Available light would have permitted traveling twenty-four hours per day because the season of no nights had arrived.

The law of supply and demand in the arctic exists much the same as it does in the more populated regions further south. In both areas the supply of problems far exceeds the demand. After an eight-hour sleep break we awakened to find that the northern elements had obliterated our tracks. Although the wind had subsided, a heavy ground fog made it impossible for us to obtain our directions from the position of the sun. We were lost.

Tumuk made me aware of our dilemma by pointing at himself, pointing at me, uttering the English word, "Come," and then pointing in all directions.

I couldn't determine if he was asking me which way we came or which way we should go. But in any event, his meaning came through perfectly clear. He had a problem. He didn't know east from west.

Carefully I studied the landscape while the native bled off his excess emotion by almost continuous laughter, waiting for me to provide a clue as to which way was which. I pointed to the rocks that normally enable a native to find his way as effectively as street signs enable a city dweller to find an address. He shook his head. His high peak of excitement the previous day may have caused him to neglect locating any markers. I looked again. Since snow suitable for igloo building was difficult to find during the melting season we were using a tent. The tent provided an obvious answer. We had pitched it with the door facing south. To Tumuk a commercial tent was an unfamiliar convenience. He had obviously failed to notice the directions when I laid it out for erection.

I drew a line in the snow marking it with arrows to indicate the west. Then I drew the tent just below the line. After I had spent some three minutes explaining my logic the native grinned from ear to ear. He had the picture.

Still, even though our position was firmly established, Tumuk refused to break camp. In answer to my signs indicating collapsing the tent and packing the sleigh, he pointed to the overcast sky and covered his eyes. Then he pointed to himself and to me and swung his arms to indicate a big circle. To make certain I completely understood he repeated the procedure three more times.

I spent the next five hours staring into a fogbank while we waited for traveling visibility. As a boy I had always wanted to go tenting — I had envisioned joys such as sitting beside an open tent door and deciding whether to sunbathe, fish or swim. But the tenting and related activities I envisioned certainly differed from those I was now experiencing. I found I had no need to choose. The sun remained well hidden above the fog. Without first finding a suitable swimming hole and then removing the heavy thickness of ice forming a cover it would have been impossible to swim. And I lacked the patience, the skill and the endurance to catch fish in the manner Curly had displayed while he secured nourishment during our deer hunt.

After five hours the wait finally ended. The mist cleared and we could see the sky. The period of the year had arrived when the sun circled at a constant height in the heavens. Around midnight, as if to avoid colliding with the north star, it dipped to the horizon at the midpoint of its northern arc. It now shone from this low position. Not only could I confirm that the twelve thirty showing on my watch indicated half past midnight, but I could also confirm with certainty that the tent door faced south.

Tumuk was fully aware of the time. Nevertheless, we broke camp and started on our way. There were two reasons for breaking camp in the middle of the night; the dogs did not require further rest, and during the season of the midnight sun, travel in the cool of the night is less tiring than travel during the heat of the day. In a region where the high temperature in mid-summer seldom rises above sixty degrees Fahrenheit, using the cool of a spring night to avoid the daytime heat sounds like an excellent solution for a problem that does not exist. However, in some circumstances, the hindsight of experience far surpasses the foresight of logic. I had already learned that in the arctic, these circumstances prevailed ninety-nine per cent of the time.

At nine that morning we pitched the tent. The monotonous waiting and the arduous traveling had combined to turn the previous night into a long, hard, tiring day. I crawled into my sleeping bag and immediately dozed off. By ten o'clock I woke up wet with sweat. Our tent of treated canvas, dark against the undulating sea of white, absorbed not only the direct rays of the sun but the reflections from the snow as well.

The sea provided the Inuit with food. It also provided them with their preferred travel causeways during the long winters and short summers. Only absolute necessity caused the Inuit to use the overland route. Such absolute necessity had caused Tumuk to rush ashore at the first opening he found that would permit a crossing of the open stretch of water. Consequently, we were now traveling through country unexplored by white men and unfrequented by natives.

The Inuit could easily have pinpointed our exact location if we had been following the coastal route. But now he had no blazed trail or familiar landmarks to guide him. Our hope of reaching our intended destination depended entirely on our ability to navigate and make an accurate estimate of the distance we had traveled. If we traveled too far before turning, we would be west of Wager Inlet and could wander forever without finding our intended journey's end. The position of the sun and the drifts and ridges in the snow that were formed by the prevailing winds enabled us to travel in the proper direction. Recognition of the overland trail to Wager from Repulse would confirm we had managed to correctly estimate the distance we had traveled. We could have been the first people to travel over this portion of the stone-studded plateau and I could certainly have been the first white man. However, the thrill of possibly treading where white man had never trod before was not the phenomenon that caused me to reach a highly emotional state. Instead I contracted the native's encompassing uneasiness. I began to wonder how many other white men had been in a similar situation and never had the opportunity to eventually tell their fellow *kabloonas* about it.

After three days of travel that required greater than usual amounts of tugging and braking, Tumuk suddenly relaxed. He pointed to a nearby heap of rocks and excitedly explained something. His happy expression and actions led me to assume that our path had crossed the well-marked trail between Repulse Bay and Wager Inlet. We could have arrived at a section of our now idle trap line. But my lack of experience and inability in distinguishing one arctic rock from the billions of other arctic rocks scattered over the landscape made it impossible for me to prove or disprove my assumption. We altered course and the going got tougher. Nevertheless, we were two happier wanderers than we had been for the past three days. Not only was I acquiring fragments of the Inuit tongue and assimilating bits of their culture, my emotions were in complete empathy with those of the native.

Our travel pace seemed to quicken. The dogs required less prompting from Tumuk's whip. Sleigh dogs seldom behaved in such a manner without sufficient reason. The reason in this case became readily apparent. The barking of other dogs informed us that we were in the vicinity of an Inuit camp. We crossed a hummock and saw a solitary igloo nestled in a snow bank on the south side of a rise. I soon found myself being introduced to Tukeyuk and his family. Tukeyuk's family consisted of his wife and six-month-old son.

As soon as the formal greetings were completed I took the Primus, entered the igloo and began to make tea. My deer-hunting expedition had taught me, among other things, to make certain that the grub box always contained a substantial supply of flour, baking powder and lard. This not only provided a variation from the natives' meat and fish diet; it also ensured a supply of emergency rations if the trip took longer than anticipated. Tumuk entered the igloo with my baking ingredients and arranged for Tukeyuk's wife to whip up a bunch of bannock. While she was hand-mixing the mess of flour, water and lard, the infant in her parka hood pouch indicated his need to visit the bathroom. She lifted the youngster from his cosy nest, held him over the igloo floor and let nature take its course. Her forefinger served well as paper while she performed the necessary wiping chores. The relieved infant was returned to his parka-hood cradle. With a couple of handfuls of snow the mother covered all traces of the function. She half-heartedly wiped her hand against the snow bench and resumed mixing bannock.

Eskimos shared. When a traveler with food visited a camp where food was scarce everyone in camp ate well from his larder. If a hungry traveler visited the camp, he shared their meager provisions. Since hunting had been poor lately, the Tukeyuk household were without food. When we arrived we had two and a half frozen seals to feed the dogs. The next evening when we left, we had one and a dozen dog-sized bites.

Whether it was freshly killed or frozen, seal could be eaten raw. The feasters seated themselves on the snowbench. With the entire animal hauled to within their easy reach, the feast began. Each native picked up a snow knife and hacked off the wanted amount. Our hostess had no cooking or serving problems — her guests continued to chew and belch until their visibly extended stomachs could hold no more.

The natives considered our frozen, ready-to-eat dog food far more palatable than the concoction of flour, grease, baking powder and water that had to be cooked. This left me free to gorge on the overly generous supply of bannock to my heart's content. Unfortunately my memories of the sanitary arrangements in the igloo kitchen took the edge off my appetite. Since only an empty larder prevented the Inuit from eating heartily, my finicky approach provided them with mealtime entertainment. They had something to joke about, and they laughed uproariously.

That night an empty tobacco tin serving as a chamber pot was passed from sleeping bag to sleeping bag. I noticed that the natives paid little attention to either the seal or the bannock as they emptied the contents. The next evening when we resumed our journey, I had no difficulty ignoring the possibility of being hungry before the end of the trip. I actually felt comfort in adhering to the native custom of leaving the remnants of a feast behind.

All night, while cracking his whip, untangling the traces, lugging on the steep upgrades, braking on the steep descents and taking care of any other dog team driving chores, Tumuk hummed a three-note tune to himself.

Before we broke camp the following morning, my trail boss made some navigational calculations. He counted on his fingers and made some marks in the snow. He repeated his calculations twice more.

"We will travel south to the coast," he spoke in Inuit and translated by gestures.

Within three hours we reached the head of the series of dry gulches and ravines that sloped from the center plateau down to the coast. Soon we began traveling along the smooth roadway at the bottom of one of these ravines. After about three miles I completely adjusted to riding on the sleigh, rather than providing assistance to the dogs. Then suddenly, Tumuk recognized his surroundings. We abandoned the easy route and changed to a course that took us uphill, downhill and across the gulches. But before I could adjust to the pull-ahead, pull-back method of travel we again changed course. The fourth gulley served as a channel for one of the arctic's many unnamed creeks and Tumuk turned upstream.

Barking dogs could be heard in the distance. The team surged forward at a pace bordering on that which Tumuk had raised them to during our final seconds on the ice floe. Soon other dogs appeared on the banks of our sunken causeway and communicated in angry tones with Tumuk's team. I looked for a harpoon, a *komutik* standing on end, or some other indication of an igloo's location. I could see no markers of any kind.

We came to a frozen-over waterfall and stopped. Tumuk jumped from the sleigh and beckoned me to follow. At the edge of the waterfall he pushed aside a deerskin and we entered an ice-walled cavern.

Here Nooloo and his family made their home. Every year they took advantage of the fact that eight to ten months of freezing weather produced a giant igloo from the cascade. They had no need to crawl through the egress. Standing upright they could walk into a dwelling area, twelve feet long, eight feet wide and a ceiling fifteen feet above the frozen floor.

During the summer the high banks above the falls rigidly confined the water to its channel. When it reached the sheer cliff that initiated the drop, the sudden release from this confinement forced the water to tumble to the sides as well as fall in the direction of the current. Every autumn, when Nooloo prepared his provided-by-nature shelter for a winter abode, he found it necessary to chop an entrance through one of these side walls. Then, in order to fashion a snow bench and provide a packed snow floor covering, blocks of snow had to be carried in.

As I entered, Nooloo's wife and two children were sitting on the well-used snow bench. They wore grins stretching from ear to ear as they stared at the small portion of my freckled face that my red beard failed to hide. Their interested gazes left little doubt that I had the distinction of being the first red-headed human they had seen.

The furnishings of the igloo were sparse. All Nooloo's hunting gear, including his sleigh, rested against one wall of the ice cavern. A flat rock served as a table. The rock reached the full length of the shelter and obviously formed at least the top layer and possibly the substratum of the earth's surface. From Mrs. Nooloo's position on the snow bench a seal-oil lamp had been placed within easy reach, close to the edge of the table. The lamp consisted of a saucer carved from soapstone filled with seal oil. A wick had been fashioned from arctic moss. The wick circled the inner rim of the saucer and produced a somewhat languid flame. A ring of carefully selected stones held a pan of water just above this reluctant blaze. The water barely simmered. Nooloo's wife picked up a paddle made from walrus tusk and patted the wick. A slightly improved flame rewarded her efforts. She seemed satisfied that the lamp had now reached its ultimate output, but obviously it would never generate sufficient heat to raise the temperature of the slightly simmering water to boiling point.

I brought in the Primus stove and kettle, boiled some water and made tea. Tumuk loaned the Nooloo family his cup. The father drank first, then passed the cup to his wife who in turn, gave each of the children a sip. Our host's "thank you" was both spontaneous and in English.

Thank you, I soon learned, formed his entire English vocabulary. However, his facial expression enabled him to convey that his thank you was absolutely genuine. Additional words were certainly not required.

We spent the twelve-hour resting time sharing the luxury of Nooloo's spacious igloo. I felt tired and slept most of the day. Tumuk, however, visited every minute of our stay. Whenever I awakened he and Nooloo were drinking tea, talking and laughing. I understood little of what the natives said but it sounded as if Nooloo had little food for his family and none at all for his dogs. When we left that evening I received definite proof that my knowledge of the Inuit language was improving. We had arrived at Nooloo's camp with a complete seal and sufficient remnants of a previous seal to give the dogs one feeding. We left with half a seal.

The handful of tea leaves that the natives brewed and rebrewed during the day were carefully spread on the rock table. After they were thoroughly dried they would make fine smoking. The pipe Nooloo fashioned from walrus tusk already lay beside the leaves, waiting to be put to use.

One final kettle of tea had to be brewed and drank before Tumuk decided not to linger longer. We began the necessary preparations for our departure. For some reason our host and his family disregarded the usual native custom of ignoring departing guests, and all were on hand to assist in some way. Nooloo helped harness the dogs. His wife and youngsters made certain our traveling luggage was firmly lashed to the *komutik*. They all exchanged spoken good wishes with Tumuk and smiles with me.

To avoid climbing a twenty-foot cliff we made a short detour. Then we followed the stream to its source. I found it provided drainage to a small lake. We turned to the west and took advantage of a couple of miles of easy traveling. Tumuk now displayed the confidence of a man who knows exactly where he is and where he is going. Obviously he was given a verbal route map by Nooloo. In fact, we were traveling over Nooloo's inland hunting and fishing area. All too soon we had traveled the full length of the lake and commenced traveling over the rough terrain. We tugged, lugged and braked over the bumpy ground until five o'clock the next morning. Suddenly Tumuk pointed in the direction of the coast. "Mail," he said.

But something of greater interest than mail caught and held the native's attention. Fresh polar bear tracks crossed our path. My trail boss made a quick revision to the trip's priority list. We abandoned the mail run and our scheduled rest time; polar bear hunting became the order of the day.

With the skill that comes only from practice the native rapidly unloaded the sleigh, then lashed the bearskin ground sheet and the rifles back on.

We started the hunt. The fresh scent of the animal provided the only guidance the dogs required. It also provided the only guidance the dogs would heed. Eagerly they rushed forward. We clung to the bouncing, jolting sled. After crossing two gullies, the trail turned and followed a third gully toward the sea. The dogs began to bark madly. Our quarry could be seen casually sauntering along less than half a mile ahead.

We were well within shooting range before the beast acknowledged his company. He started to run. Tumuk released all his huskies except the lead dog. He upset the *komutik* and anchored it firmly between two boulders. Quickly the dogs caught up to the bear and began circling and jumping at the huge animal. The beast reared up on its hind legs and began to cuff at its tormentors.

The Inuit and myself raced forward with fully loaded rifles. As we approached, one of the bear's enormous paws made contact with a dog. Before it could manage even a quick yelp the canine traveled a good thirty feet through the air, landing on the snow a lifeless mass of torn fur and broken bones.

We emptied the magazines of both rifles without making any visible effect on the bear. Then, while we were reloading, the animal fell. Tumuk motioned me to approach with caution. But a little probing on his part indicated we had a polar bear skin for the taking.

We now had an adequate supply of dog food. Also, since a second dog had received a cuff from the mighty animal, we had two fewer dogs to feed.

Tumuk sat on the downed bear. Until now I had failed to notice that not only had he left his sled armed with a rifle, but he had carried his whip as well. The huskies also became suddenly aware that he had brought along his emphatic means of control. They sullenly drew back from their intended feast and stood waiting just beyond the range of the stinging lash.

I returned to free the sleigh and allow the lead dog to lug it up to the rest of the pack. We loaded our prize and returned to our tent and other abandoned possessions.

Arrival at the mail cache was the most important aspect of the trip for me. However, the native had priorities that differed greatly from mine. Right now his number-one priority consisted of skinning a polar bear.

While I erected the tent, Tumuk gave his full attention to the skinning operation. As he worked he helped himself to any savory tidbits he uncovered. He would stuff raw meat into his mouth until a portion of the last handful remained dangling outside his lips. Then using an *ooloo* (a short-handled knife with an extremely sharp semi-circular blade) he cut off the overflow, closed his mouth and began chewing. By the time he finished skinning the animal his face was caked with bear blood.

When I had all our equipment safely inside the tent I made tea and cooked myself some bannock. With the supply of fresh meat the native would shun my *kabloona*'s food.

After several hours' rest, Tumuk handed me a second disappointment. When we broke camp we did not proceed immediately to the mail cache but began retracing our steps to Nooloo's camp. My personal wishes were certainly not to pay a second visit within three days to a family of starving Eskimos. But, when in Rome one should do as the Romans do; when in Inuit land it was just as important to do as the Inuit do. I was in Inuit land. Without any objections on my part, we went to visit Nooloo.

The dogs found pulling the *komutik* heavy lugging. Not only were there now fewer dogs to do the pulling, but the mad chase had taken its toll on the mud shoes that provided smooth sliding over the snow. Several chunks of mud and ice had been knocked off. The jagged edges left by these missing pieces created a braking effect. Even though most of the road consisted of good sledding, we arrived at the frozen-over waterfall with an extremely tired dog team.

The entire Nooloo family welcomed us so enthusiastically, I felt like a wealthy relative who had just returned from a couple of years' absence. After tea was brewed and two cups each consumed, Tumuk began to tell his fellow natives about the bear. Our hosts, of course, received a good portion of our prize. When we left Tumuk had two of Nooloo's dogs harnessed with his team. At some later date they would be returned.

During the coolest part of the night the natives repaired the broken mud shoes. In lieu of earth, they fashioned a paste from a pot of oatmeal porridge. I had noticed the neatly tied bag of rolled oats in our grub box and until then considered it had been added in case we required emergency rations. That we would carry a repair kit for sled runners had never occurred to me.

The huskies, like any other dog, will eat any edible object they happen to find. Normally Tumuk let his dogs bed down untethered. But to avoid fighting, both his and Nooloo's team were tethered at distances sufficient to prevent them from inflicting wounds on each other. Fortunately, sufficient inedible tethers were found to secure both teams. The runners remained intact.

That evening we began to retrace our steps over the short route that was turning into a well-used trail. With the benefit of freshly iced runners, a brief traveling period brought us to our previous camping site. We rested for several hours before reloading the sleigh and finally beginning the last short lap to the mail cache. Although my eagerness to open my mail greatly influenced my reasoning, I still accepted the time consumed in reloading the sleigh as being time well spent. Even in the spring, arctic blizzards can be sudden, severe and long-lasting. Making camp at the first sign of a blizzard, especially when you have a supply of food, provides for a fair chance of survival. Wandering aimlessly and looking for an abandoned camp site provides for little chance of survival.

As if to mark our journey's end a monument of snow blocks was erected where the canyon met the coast. Tumuk slashed an opening in the cairn with his snow knife and there was our mail.

Eagerly I stripped the canvas wrappings from a cardboard carton. I carefully began to untie the string that held the carton together. It would be required to rebind the package after I removed my personal mail. The knots were tight and difficult to undo. I found the delay most frustrating. But when I finally managed to open the carton, I met an even greater frustration. The box contained a well-stuffed government mail bag, firmly secured with an official lock. I did not have a key. Still, both Tumuk and myself had sharp snow knives. Although I would be breaking the law by cutting into a locked sack of mail, the odds that I would ever be charged with the felony were about one in ten thousand. And those odds would only take effect if some of the mail was lost after it was removed from the protection of the bag. The possibility of prosecution because of lost mail was extremely remote. But the possibility of strained relations between me and my fellow trader over lost or damaged mail were very real. Reluctantly I decided that the opening ceremonies should be postponed until I arrived back at Repulse.

I rewrapped the mail in the waterproof canvas and Tumuk lashed it to the sleigh. I had fulfilled my main purpose in making the trip. Now, like the youngster who has just received his present at a Christmas concert, I wanted to go home. Even the thought of a supply of tobacco at Wager failed to provide me with any needed encouragement to continue the trip.

But, regardless of my desires, I was in a situation where a pre-arranged schedule dictated where I would go. We resumed the journey to Wager. My glimpse of the shoreline left no doubt in my mind that travel by the coastal route would have met all arctic safety require-ments. But obviously Tumuk had decided to continue with an overland route. His actions gave every indication that he did not know for certain where he was going. He did, however, know where he was not going —back on the salt sea ice.

Nevertheless, travel over an unknown, inland trail finally brought us to the same destination we would have reached by traveling over the well-known, shoreline route. We arrived at Wager Inlet.

Wager Inlet was once a completely self-contained trading post. A set of three buildings, consisting of a house, a store and a warehouse, were nestled in a small valley . As manager of the outpost, Dick had the opportunity of living the life of a native or living the life of a trader. Five minutes in the settlement proved to be sufficient to determine which lifestyle Dick considered to be the good life. The people that came to greet us came from the warehouse; they did not live in the house.

The warehouse consisted of one huge room with a back porch. It resembled an immense igloo with a snow tunnel entrance. At one end of the room two double beds were placed end to end. Dick and his family seated themselves on one bed while his brother and family sat on the other. Individual caribou-hide sleeping bags were placed on the bare mattresses, marking each member's allotted spot on this giant substitute snow bench. An overturned packing box and a wooden bench along one wall completed the furnishings in the room. A Primus stove and seal-oil lamp shared the surface of the packing box. Other than the seal-oil lamp, no heating arrangements existed. This was Dick's summer quarters. During the cold days of winter the families lived in a couple of cozy igloos.

Somewhere the natives had acquired a spring-powered gramophone and six records. In honor of my visit the machine was placed in the middle of the floor and each record played at least twice.

Through a series of gestures, supplemented by Pidgin English, Dick's wife managed to convey to me that she wished me to dance with her daughter in the white man's style. One look at the expression on the girl's face told me that she was reluctant to abide by her mother's wishes. Tumuk immediately volunteered to be my dancing partner. He and I foxtrotted through two renditions of "Walking My Baby Back Home." Foxtrotting is not the ideal method of resting up after a week on the trail.

As Tom had suggested, when it came time to retire I took my sleeping bag and retreated to the solitude of the house. The house consisted of a kitchen, living room and two bedrooms. The dwelling was not completely empty of furnishings. Three chairs, a table, a coal and wood range, a dresser and two single beds complete with mattresses still remained. I selected the bedroom with the dresser and laid my sleeping bag on the bed. Immediately, I had company. Tumuk and the fourteen-year-old girl came to visit. The girl had washed her face.

Tumuk attempted to convey some sort of message to me. Among other things he inquired if I would feel cold during the night. I also ascertained that the half-dozen wristwatches on the dresser belonged to the girl. Finally in desperation, he carried Mrs. Crawford's twenty-two into the bedroom and pointed first to the rifle and then to the girl. I shook my head. As I started to explain that the rifle did not belong to me I suddenly realized I would be asked for some other item. I let my flat denial stand. Holding hands and looking both relieved and happy, they left. My answer may not have pleased the mother; but it delighted both the girl and my traveling companion.

I lit the Primus stove and heated a kettle of snow water. I removed the irritating beard that had started to give me a bad case of itchy skin. Washing my dirty face made me feel so good that, even though the temperature of the house stood below freezing, I heated more water and treated myself to a sponge bath. My extra shirt served remarkably well as a towel. Then I placed it on the drying rack that was still hanging over the kitchen range. As I was unaccustomed to housekeeping chores, the thought of dusting the rack first never occurred to me. But since very little dust is emitted by the arctic snow, no telltale streak on the garment resulted from my oversight.

When the natives visited they felt little, if any, compulsion to be up and moving early in the morning. Dick, being an Inuit, lived by Inuit customs. So although stock-taking was the order of the day, I slept late. Tumuk and his young friend arrived well past ten o'clock to make certain I had survived the night. I accompanied them to the warehouse-turned-living quarters.

Dick's wife had coffee and bannock prepared. Without awakening me, the natives had somehow spirited the table and a couple of chairs from the house to the warehouse. The table was now laid with a clean linen table napkin set with heavy porcelain dishes and steel cutlery. I certainly felt like the honored guest.

Stock-taking with Dick was easy. He knew without counting how many of each item he had on hand — my count merely verified his figures. He had his own way of naming the various items in my language. For example he described ladies' fleece-lined bloomers as "pants like Nellie wears."

But although the stock-taking was fast and easy, it was not without its disappointments. Stock items which the natives seldom purchased were carried only in token quantities at Wager Inlet. As tobacco proved to be one of these items, the small supply was exhausted by Christmas. Consequently, the fringe benefit both Tom and I had hoped for didn't materialize.

Even though a few hours proved to be sufficient time to complete the stock count, the evening failed to see us depart for home. I began to have thoughts about a sharp knife and a locked mail bag. After all, a little reading would certainly pass the time while Tumuk visited. However, I spent the night sleeping.

Around eleven o'clock the next morning my guide and his fourteen-year-old playmate decided to go rabbit hunting. He insisted that I accompany them. The girl did not even carry a rifle. Finally we saw a rabbit two hundred yards in the distance, stopping to survey the countryside. Tumuk motioned for me to shoot. Although the arctic hare was well out of range I didn't argue. My shot appeared to raise a puff of snow just short of the animal. The flight of the bullet had been true and almost strong enough to carry the full distance. Mrs. Crawford's twenty-two was an excellent rifle. Obtaining game could not have been the purpose of the trip because we immediately returned to the post. Upon our arrival at Wager, we reverted to the age-old custom of sleeping at night and performing daytime tasks during the day. The safari could have been to fill in part of the day by proving that I had need for the rifle.

Around ten o'clock the next evening we departed from Wager Inlet. The girl and her mother were on hand to bid us farewell. Dick and the rest of the natives followed the Inuit custom of greeting arriving visitors and ignoring them when they left. Tumuk was in good spirits and I was in a happy mood. As soon as we arrived at Repulse with the mail I could begin reading those long-awaited letters.

While I busied myself taking stock with Dick I discovered he treated his outpost manager's duties as a Saturday afternoon job. He provided for his family by fishing and hunting. His stipend assured that he would have the necessary supply of shells and traps. His post allowance insured he would have a supply of tea and hardtack for any fellow native who came to trade. The trading post guaranteed that his family would have many visitors.

Hunting and fishing required Dick to be away from the post a considerable portion of the time. This did not cut down on his efficiency as a manager. If an Inuit family came to trade during his absence, one of Dick's family members would unlock the store and let the customers browse. Trading usually took a minimum of two days, so waiting until Dick returned caused no problems. Often the major part of the trading was completed in his absence and only the reckoning and recording remained to be done upon his return.

Dick preferred to continue along the native life pattern, meaning that he avoided following the line of least resistance. He made his choice through his sense of values.

The choice meant an arduous life, but it was not without its compensations. It was based on co-operation rather than competition. A complete lack of any criminal element balanced the lack of materialistic comforts. Mistrust was unknown. It was a system that worked because all members of the community worked. They were entirely self-sufficient.

Snow made houses. Sealskin made boots, mitts and kayaks. Caribou hides made clothing. Trade goods obtained for fox pelts made life a little easier but certainly could not be considered necessary. Rifles provided an aid to kill polar bears but it was not unknown to hear of a native killing one with a snow knife tied to a pole. The major supply of food consisted of traveling out on the sea ice and harpooning a seal through its breathing hole. Dick, in addition to others I met, proved that the Inuit had little difficulty developing other talents. Obviously they preferred to live a life in which the only fighting consisted of a continuous battle with the natural elements.

We had traveled for approximately two hours when Tumuk produced, seemingly from nowhere, a soup ladle carved from a muskox horn. By diligently scraping with his ooloo he removed a good portion of the half-inch layer of grease that encrusted the object, then handed the ladle to me as a present.

Even though we traveled through the night the sun glared from the sky and reflected from the snow. My face sunburned and my glasses froze to the tender skin of my blistered face. But I fared better than Tumuk. On the fourth night of the journey, despite the fact he wore native sunglasses (which consisted of two peepholes in a mask fashioned from walrus tusk), Tumuk became snowblind.

Suddenly my status changed from that of a pampered passenger with nothing to do but lug, tug and brake to that of a hard-working teamster. To my other duties I now had the tasks of cracking the whip and swearing at the dogs added.

During my boyhood, the Saturday afternoon movie in the local picture palace created a fad among my age group for making whips. The rich kids used leather shoelaces for lashes. The rest of us cut a length of leather from the back of a worn-out mitt or any other piece of discarded leather that could be used for the purpose. A few well-tied knots to obtain sufficient length were quite acceptable, while a stick of green willow the correct length made an excellent handle. Like my playmates I soon became an expert at whip cracking. Consequently, I anticipated no difficulty in handling the Inuit version of the friendly persuader.

I let the lash trail behind the sleigh. Then I swung the handle and waited for the flipped lash to snap over the center of the team. But when my whip-cracking action was completed, most of the lash still trailed behind the sleigh. The dogs' animal instinct told them it was safe to relax so they slowed from a gallop to a trot. I jumped from the sleigh and tried again. This time I met with greater success. Instead of having the majority of the lash trailing behind me, I managed to wrap a good portion of it around my body and the dogs slowed from a trot to a walk.

It's easier to handle a thirty-inch length of leather than a thirty-foot length of sealhide thong. I tried again. This time I heard the lash slide against my parka hood just before it wrapped itself around my neck. Improvement came with every try. I am certain I would have soon mastered the art of Inuit whip-handling. But by now, three of the dogs had stopped altogether. I looped the lash around the handle until I had about four free feet. With this persuader I began to persuade the dogs on an individual basis to commence moving again. But for every dog I started two stopped. We were going nowhere fast. Apparently the dogs, well aware of a change in drivers, decided to establish a few changes of their own. Already they were well on their way to establishing that the driver was no longer in charge.

Tumuk came to my rescue. Now that he had left Wager Inlet he wished to get home to his wife and baby. He took the whip and, with both eyes still closed, managed to crack it over the center of the team. As soon as the dogs heard their master's voice they surged forward. From the first-aid kit I gave Tumuk a bandage that he used to cover his eyes. Since I could see and he could crack the whip, driving the team became a combination effort. I would point the whip tip to the dog needing encouragement and he would take over from there.

We were following a well-marked trail between Wager Inlet and Repulse Bay. But following a native trail required the ability to read the markers. I might just as well have been blazing a new trail that linked no place with nowhere. Fortunately, the lead dog sensed that she was going home and had little difficulty smelling out the route to get there. Judging by the time of day, the position of the sun and the drifts that formed from the prevailing winds, I knew we continued to travel in the right direction. My main guiding chore consisted of yanking the front end of the sled sideways to prevent it from becoming snagged on one of the numerous boulders.

Since I lacked the expertise to catch and re-harness the dogs, they were deprived of their daytime sleep. With the full support of Tumuk I elected to travel day and night. Every four hours we took a break — the first three breaks lasted for one hour. During this time we made tea and fed ourselves. The fourth break lasted for two hours which provided sufficient time to feed both man and dogs. At feeding time each dog received his portion of bear meat. Using the whip handle as a club I made certain that the rest of the team stayed away until the served dog had the portion in its mouth. After that, it became the dog's responsibility to keep it. We traveled for seventy-two hours without stopping to sleep.

When we were within a half day's travel from the post, Tumuk decided he could stand to have his eyes uncovered. As soon as the native saw the familiar landmarks he realized our trip was nearly completed. Immediately he asked for a souvenir. I suddenly became aware that the lack of hand gestures during the past three days had forced a crash course in Inuit on me. I couldn't carry on a conversation in the native tongue, but by using carefully chosen words Tumuk could convey his thoughts to me. And his wish for a memento came through loud and clear. Other than the clothes I wore, the remainder of my traveling gear belonged to the Crawfords. Fortunately, the native was easily satisfied. We exchanged belts. For my commercial cowhide variety with its shiny nickel-plated buckle I received a durable sealhide product with a buckle from which the nickel plating had long since disappeared.

When we reached the southern coast of Repulse Bay Tumuk attempted to turn his dogs to the west in order to avoid crossing over any ice. But the dogs had a mind of their own. Although Tumuk's eyes still bothered him, he reluctantly guided the team through the barrier of ice along the shore. Then he again covered his eyes. But even though only half his face was exposed it was sufficient to show his anxiety as we rushed over the frozen bay.

By the time we reached the post the list of things I intended to do before I slept became the list of things I intended to do as soon as I woke up. Even the mail I had been so eager to read was forgotten. I stretched out on the bed fully clothed and slept for eight hours.

Upon awakening I immediately thumbed through my mail. I was disappointed. When I had arrived at Repulse Bay I had written to my family, my friends and my acquaintances to advise them that the next mail I received would be a year later when the supply ship made its annual visit. As a result, none of them had written. I glanced at the letter advising me that I'd been paying unemployment insurance for the past six months, my wage balance and other items that were of little interest at the time. Then I washed, shaved, ate a good meal and spent another four hours sleeping away the disappointment generated by failure to receive any eagerly awaited mail.

The Long Days

The twenty-four-hour daily sunshine meant the temperature remained above freezing for longer periods each day. The snow melted and the igloos disintegrated, causing the post natives to once again erect their dilapidated, animal-hide tents. Spring had arrived.

Because of the permafrost, water from the melting snow could not seep into the ground. Every slight depression in the terrain served as a collection basin and the landscape became dotted with overflowing pools. However, water's natural tendency to flow downhill soon created numerous little streams that melted their way to the coast and provided drainage for these pools. But even long after the pools and streams had dried up, the bay remained ice-bound.

Tom and the Fathers from the mission began transmitting orders for the items they wished the luxury-laden supply ship to bring them. I didn't wish to have any merchandise brought; I wanted only to be transported out. Once I arrived in the industrialized portion of the country, I could select my purchases in person. Even the prospects of the good returns a trapline would provide in the coming year failed to deter me from my resolve to be on the next departing boat. But before the boat could depart, it had to arrive — and waiting for that boat's arrival made the short summer seem long.

As soon as the snow melted Tom introduced me to one of his summer season boredom-killing projects. The previous year he had started work on an ice well. Although the natives had no difficulty in eating and digesting raw and sometimes partly fermented meat, the

Crawfords insisted their meat be both fresh and cooked. During the short summer period, even freshly killed seal soon began to spoil. Although the frigid weather soon halted the decaying process, a supply of ice or some other method of refrigeration would prove beneficial during the few weeks of mild temperatures.

Digging at Repulse Bay entailed using a pick to chop approximately the top three inches of frozen ground. Attempting to dig a deeper layer was like attempting to dig a hole in set concrete. Experience had taught Tom that at least two days of thawing were necessary before another layer could be excavated. This was the second summer of work on the project and when I left Repulse, at least one more summer would be required before the ice well was completed.

The warmer weather meant that open salt water remained open. The seals found that they no longer had to break an icy crust to keep their breathing holes in operating condition. Even the edges of the holes began to melt and erode. The mammals took advantage of these larger holes to ease up through them, lie on top of the ice and bask in the sun. Once on top of the ice they would raise their heads at regular intervals and look for danger. Every seal had its own head-raising cadence. But this cadence was so exact a clock could have been set by it.

To the Inuit, mimicking a seal on top of the ice came easily. They slid themselves over the frozen bay on a small sleigh. With a regular cadence they would raise their heads, not to look for danger, but to determine how close they had managed to creep to the seal. So great were their stalking skills, it was possible for them to reach a proximity that permitted spearing the animal with a harpoon. However, modern technology and the availability of rifles had rendered such skills and patience unnecessary. Nevertheless, before shooting they still edged their way close enough to see the whites of their quarry's eyes. Not every stalking meant a kill. After as much as an hour's creeping something could alert the seal and, by sliding back through the breathing hole, it would retreat to its under-ice security. When this happened the native located another basking seal and began stalking again. If he made a kill he feasted. If his hunt proved to be unsuccessful he fasted. But on the morrow, he would again make every effort to feast.

Tom decided that until I had tried my hand at this type of seal hunting, my education would be incomplete. Armed with his small sleigh, his thermos filled with coffee, his thirty-thirty rifle and his telescope, we set out.

If luck is required for a hunter to sight his game then luck was certainly with us that day. Before we were a full four miles from shore we spotted at least five seals waiting on the ice. Through the telescope we determined that a large bearded seal was the nearest animal to us. The distinctive shape of this animal's flippers earned it the name "square flipper."

I was dispatched to ride on the small sled, get within range and do the shooting. Tom remained behind to watch the action through his telescope and give any necessary instructions. I had barely crawled to within rifle range of the animal when he signaled me to shoot. I took careful aim. Through the rifle sights I saw what I felt was an Inuit doing his imitation of a creeping seal. I lowered the rifle to take a better look. Tom shouted at me to shoot. It was too late. As I began to take aim again the seal reached its breathing hole and slid from view.

Tom came running up. "Why didn't you shoot?" he scolded. Both the expression on his face and the tone of his voice registered his disgust at my hesitation. I explained my reason. He handed me the telescope. A quick glance through the glass was sufficient to make me realize I had been ridiculously cautious.

The square flipper was one of several seals. Tom now took his turn at crawling until he reached rifle range. Unfortunately, his shot failed to kill the animal instantly and, although possibly wounded, it managed to slide back into the water.

At Repulse hen eggs were unknown and breakfast often consisted of ham and eggs without the eggs. But in the spring we had a change of diet. Although ice that was sturdy enough to bear the weight of an eight-hundred-pound square flipper still covered the salt water, gulls arrived and began nesting. Three miles from the post, towards the narrow neck of the bay, a series of sheer cliffs formed the shoreline. The gulls considered the ledges on the cliff faces to be an ideal nesting ground. The chicks hatched. When the mother gull considered her offspring were old enough to leave the nest, she made certain they left. She pushed them out. If they couldn't fly they would flutter the hundred feet or so down to the water — they would always float.

Because I weighed a few pounds less than the senior member of the two-man staff, I was the one most frequently lowered over the edge of the cliff to pluck the eggs from the nests. But scaling a wall of sheer rock never really thrilled me; it scared me. I much preferred to be the anchor man holding the rope. The footing on the top of the cliff was far more to my liking than that on the face.

A shotgun and a box of shells were left at the post by a former manager. Tom had never accustomed himself to using a shotgun and rather than let the chance of free ammunition pass me by, I began carrying the gun on our egg-gathering expeditions.

Since we had no desire to discourage the gulls from nesting in the area we always left one egg in the nest. But on the next few visits we frequently found only the remains of a couple of egg shells. Obviously we had competition. The area was so thinly populated that wildlife had not yet become overly timid of humans. Consequently, we soon met our fellow egg thief face to face. It was a weasel. From the animal's actions it appeared that, like most weasels, he had yet to be frightened by anything. From a distance of ten yards I blasted the small animal with the ten-gauge gun. He seemed to disappear into thin air. We never saw him again, nor did we see any indication of his continued activity in the area. However, after three more trips we found ourselves forced to again eat breakfast without eggs. The icy causeway to the nesting grounds became too treacherous to use and sheer cliffs rising to heights of well over a hundred feet had to be scaled if we traveled the overland route.

Even though we used the cool of the night to walk to our egg source, the walk generated a tremendous thirst. On top of the salt ice little pockets of fresh, clear, cool water would form, providing the most refreshing drink. One evening I knelt to gulp a few mouthfuls from one of these little pools. I received a horrible surprise. A break in the ice had allowed salt water to infiltrate the clear-looking puddle. Two evenings later I could still taste the brine. Thereafter, I took time to first dip up a handful and taste it with the tip of my tongue.

The pond from which we obtained our drinking water was one of several located in close proximity to a saucer-like depression in solid rock. Possibly because the permafrost did not exist in solid rock, the water here warmed sufficiently to allow it to be used as a bathing hole. The shallow depth did not permit swimming. But it still allowed Tom and myself to have a leisurely bath after spending a couple of active hours excavating for the ice well. Since winter conditions permitted only an occasional sponge bath, the opportunity to submerge and soak was more than welcome.

On the morning of July 14, I woke up at three o'clock and noticed a definite change. Instead of the bright glow that had existed since the days of the midnight sun, the starlight and moonlight normally associated with non-daylight hours now existed. With the coming of dawn the reason for this change also became apparent. A favoring wind coupled with the outgoing tide had persuaded the broken ice to leave Repulse Bay. Summer had officially arrived. In place of the glare ice that reflected light, the constant moving waters of a green sea absorbed it.

Tom immediately took his canoe and outboard from storage. Seal-hunting season had arrived. However, the cakes of ice that still remained in the bay provided another method of obtaining the much-sought-after meat supply. When the water remained calm the seals loved to climb aboard one of these ice rafts and spend a couple of hours letting the sun warm their backs. The first indication of the waters becoming rough caused them to slide back into the sea — rumor had it that the animals were prone to seasickness.

Experience had taught Tom that, from the direction in which it was facing, a basking seal could be approached in a straight line. This method of approach failed to alarm the animal. During the period of floating floes Tom put this knowledge to practical use. Since traveling over the open water was the only method by which such an approach could be made, the canoe constituted the ideal vehicle with which to make it. The crew, consisting of Albert's Boy and myself, took up our usual seal-hunting positions. Tom handled the motor and tiller.

We made an abrupt change in our pre-shooting tactics — instead of scraping the canoe in order to create a noise that would attract the animal, we now remained perfectly quiet and still in order not to create a noise or other influence that might attract him. Just before we rammed the ice floe Tom cut the motor. That served as my signal to shoot. At the sound of the shot the canoe turned sideways to the ice. This allowed Albert's Boy to jab the animal with his harpoon, jump on to the floe and, if possible, grab a flipper. The heavy-soled mukluks provided sufficient traction to allow the native to haul a thousand-pound-square flipper into a secure position on a cake of ice.

Although the smaller harp seals also sunbathed on the ice, we preferred to stalk the larger, bearded variety. For the same effort, the latter would provide as much meat as ten of his smaller cousins. Moreover, I found the bigger seal more palatable. On the other hand, the arctic environment may have changed my taste buds to such a degree that I could now relish arctic fare.

In order to float a square flipper Albert's Boy would inflate three or more buoys. After they were secured, our kill would be towed back to the post. There we had plenty of assistance in beaching the animal before it was carefully skinned and quartered. The hide of the bearded seal was in great demand by the natives. It made strong thongs and clothing. The hide of a harp seal was never discarded; among other uses it served remarkably well for use as a buoy.

Instead of doing what any well-behaved ice pack would have done, namely get lost in the middle of Hudson's Bay, the pack that year insisted on hanging around its place of origin and making a general nuisance of itself. It began to look as if this would be one of the years in which the M.S. *Fort Severn* failed to complete its annual pilgrimage to Repulse Bay. Although a plane would fly in emergency supplies, the load of fur would have a much higher priority for passage on the outgoing trip than any discontented apprentice clerk.

Due to its close proximity to the ice, the mean temperature of the area during the summer remained very low. In fact we enjoyed such a cool summer that only for one day did the mosquitos make their presence known. But one day was sufficient. They had obviously received instructions from the boss mosquito to stage a four-hour blitz-krieg. So savage was the attack that I am certain any mosquito who returned to his home base without evidence that he inflicted a summer's misery on some hapless, warm-blooded creature, would be tortured to death with whatever bloodthirsty methods the insects use to punish their own species.

Out on the bay, away from the rocky cliffs that protected the post from the summer breeze, the wind would soon blow these tiny tormentors out of existence. But the outboard lay in pieces on the warehouse floor. If the sea turned choppy, a paddle-powered canoe would offer little protection against taking a dip in the icy water. As usual, Tom knew exactly what to do. We launched a small rowboat and leisurely rowed to the gulls' nesting grounds and back. During the spring, when we walked over the ice to the source of fresh eggs, patches of snow still covered the shaded portions of the landscape. Now, however, the snow had entirely disappeared. The green moss and bare rock so changed the scenery it appeared as if the rowboat journey had followed a different route. In one particular spot, what appeared to be a sloping four-lane highway rose from the shoreline to the top of one of the higher cliffs. Tom passed on this observation, which he had gleaned from the British Canadian Arctic Expedition. The slope had been formed by glacier ice doing a shearing job on the rock. Although such an explanation could easily account for the grade, it certainly didn't account for what appeared to be a set of ruts extending in a straight line from the top to the sea. By the time we returned, the hungry mosquitos had bedded down for another winter. At least, I never heard the buzz of their wings or felt their itchy stingers again.

The fox pelts we acquired during the winter had to be cleaned before they could be baled. Although Peter the Fox Skinner did an excellent job of scraping and cleaning away any excess fat from the inside skin of the hides, much dirt and grime still remained in the fur. Tom produced a couple of bags filled with sawdust that were retained at Repulse Bay as a fur-cleaning detergent. We dumped them into a wooden trough. The pelts were then taken and cleaned in this manu-ally operated contrivance. To free the fur from any sawdust it still retained, the pelts were hung on a clothesline. The arctic breezes would soon whisk any unanchored particles away. The clothesline stretched from the warehouse to the dwelling house and its long length created a deep sag. Several wooden props, kept in the warehouse for this once-a-year chore, were placed wherever necessary to hold the valuable hides at a height safely beyond the reach of the hungry dogs.

To the west of the house an easily climbed hill rose to an elevation that enabled me to use it as a lookout point. From this vantage point I could easily see if the ice field had moved sufficiently towards the center of the bay to allow passage of the *Fort Severn* along a coastal route. I climbed it every morning.

The hill not only afforded a view out over the bay, but over much of the surrounding countryside as well. To the west the morning sun rays reflected from the sides of a cliff. The reflections made a brilliant mixture of colors. I remembered one of my high school teachers telling the class about a similar sighting of a mixture of brilliant colors. This sighting had led to the discovery of pitchblende in the Great Bear Lake district of the North West Territories. If I couldn't get to civilization, knowledge of a pitchblende discovery would soon bring civilization to me. I scrambled across the rocks and gullies that until now I had decided were inaccessible barricades. Now, however, a destination with a purpose made a difference. I even strolled down the slope I considered to be a four-lane highway. The theory I formed about wheel ruts withstood my close inspection. At the bottom of this roadway a gully gave access to the base of my mountain of visualized riches. The pitchblende turned out to be mica. However, my dream of riches and civilization remained until I returned to the post and looked up the commercial value of my find.

On the climb to the top of the lookout hill, a plateau had been reserved for a burial ground. Since the permafrost and rocks prohibited digging, the bodies had been laid to rest on the surface and entombed with rocks and boulders. Wooden crosses, with the names of the departed carved in syllabics, marked each of the final resting spots. Remains of rifles and other hunting implements remained beside some of the older graves. Apparently, the influence generated by the Fathers from the local mission made some of the younger natives realize that you can take nothing out of this world. It was better for those who remained to put the departed's possessions to some practical, earthly use. No tools for use in the beyond lay beside the newer tombs.

One day from my lookout post I noticed what appeared to be a polar bear rearing his head on one of the islands. I cut short my usual survey of ice conditions and returned to the post. With the aid of his telescope Tom determined that the animal I had sighted was a walrus. Immediately the canoe hit the water. Albert's Boy took up his established position at the front of the boat. By the time we arrived at the island, the walrus had decided to go for a swim.

I was put ashore with a high-powered rifle. The other members of the hunting party began a systematic herding process to drive the animal into the shallow water. In deep water a fighting walrus is a dangerous foe. He dives, turns on his back and uses his tusks to rip at the underbelly of whatever is annoying him. Until the beast reached the shallow water I had instructions not to shoot. On the other hand, they fired at it with twenty-twos in an effort to drive it towards the shore. Finally, when they succeeded, Tom shouted at me to shoot. Since the beast and the canoe formed a direct line I ran to one side before firing. The men in the boat voiced their impatience. To them, fresh walrus meat warranted a greater risk than it did to me. I fired six shots altogether and had no indication if any or all of them found their mark. The others also fired from the canoe.

Finally the animal sank. When it failed to surface again the boat was carefully maneuvered to the spot where the walrus had disappeared. Even in shallow water a wounded walrus required the greatest respect. This particular walrus, however, was dead. Albert's Boy lost no time in jabbing his harpoon into the supply of fresh meat. He tossed the inflated buoy into the water to mark the spot. Tom brought the canoe closer to the shore. I waded out, without going over the tops of my mukluks and climbed aboard.

We towed the animal back to the post. The entire native population was on hand to greet us. When a white man shot a walrus it meant a prize to be shared by all. The kabloona had no use for the hide or tusks and, except for dog food, very little use for the meat. The hide made excellent soles for footwear, the tusks furnished material for harpoon heads and other much-needed items, and the flesh was a delicacy.

That night we enjoyed a supper of fried walrus liver. During the course of the meal Mrs. Crawford remarked that Curly's fifteen-year-old daughter had been informing all and sundry that *Tegaracktee* had shot a walrus. I never discovered if the youngster's statement was based on actual fact or on an assumption.

Although the odds rested slightly in favor of the ice dispensing enough to permit the *Fort Severn* to reach Repulse Bay, the odds also rested decidedly against the vessel continuing on to Igloolik. The ice between the Melville Peninsula and Baffin Island had so far resisted the lukewarm efforts of the summer season. It neither melted nor moved. To make the isolation for the post manager at Igloolik complete, the batteries for his radio had little charge left in them and the windcharger needed repairs. Since the signal from his transmitter had sufficient strength to reach Repulse Bay he transmitted his yearly balance sheet to us.

Until the batteries failed completely, he worked backwards, transmitting entries from the transactions that had enabled him to arrive at the final figure. The Hudson's Bay Company wished to keep all its profits, losses, pelt prices and other business information secret. Consequently these figures had to be decoded before they could be checked. They were then recoded and transmitted to Chesterfield Inlet. The final stage of their transmittal consisted of a radiogram from Chesterfield to Hudson Bay house in Winnipeg.

Even though Depression-era prices still existed near the sawmill sites, arctic lumber had more value than ivory. Consequently every precaution was taken to preserve the frame buildings at the trading posts. One precaution consisted of an outside paint job every second year. In the summer of 1940 the warehouse store complex was due for its coat of fresh paint. On calm days hunting seals took precedence over painting the building. But painting took number-two spot on the priority list. Although the season was short, the days were long and ample time existed for both projects.

Living in the arctic seems to awaken a dormant animal instinct in humans. During the dark days of winter we could sleep for twelve hours without stirring. Now, during the long days of summer, as little as two hours' sleep was sufficient.

One day while I was transcribing the Morse Code from a United Press news release into readable English, Tom suddenly summoned me. He was looking at the beach from the living room and felt I would enjoy the action on the water. Two Inuit were displaying their kayaking skills. They would paddle like fury. Then, when they considered they had obtained sufficient speed, they would hold the paddle in the water at the proper angle to cause the kayak to roll. Invariably, it would make a complete revolution. Since they were belted into the crafts with sealskin attached to the cockpits, no water entered the kayaks. They also wore sealskin parkas with the hoods tightly held around their faces by drawstrings so that even their bodies remained dry.

Finally the day I awaited for nearly a year arrived. While listening to the Hudson's Bay Company frequency one night we learned that the schooner was nearing the mouth of Repulse Bay. Early the next morning I climbed my lookout mountain and, sure enough, I saw a vessel making its way towards the post. I also saw the field of ice following closely on its stern. It looked as if the *Fort Severn* would be beached at Repulse Bay for the winter. But that possibility caused me little concern. Since the district manager and the ship's crew would be flown out by plane I had a fair chance of accompanying them.

As expected, the ice conditions prompted the district manager to unload the supplies for Igloolik at Repulse Bay. The freighting of these goods would be completed by dog team. A replacement manager for Igloolik and the Catholic bishop comprised the passenger list of the *Fort Severn*. The manager spent little of his time in the house at Repulse Bay. The little time he did spend, however, made him extremely envious of the family comforts Tom enjoyed.

Instead of the usual one-day stopover, the vessel remained anchored in the harbour for well over a week. Everything, including my baggage, was loaded and ready for a quick departure, day or night, whenever and if ever the ice conditions made such a sailing feasible. Every evening the district manager held a gossip session with all the Hudson's Bay Company posts located within range of the ship's transmitting equipment. Instead of laboring with the Morse Code dots and dashes, the extra power of the ship's batteries allowed for the use of a microphone. However, the extra electrical power on board the ship did not aid the transmitters located at the various posts. Replies came back in Morse Code. In order to back up the receiving, I visited the ship every evening during this gossip session. The frequency of these visits increased my social life at Repulse Bay by five hundred per cent.

To avoid beaching at low tide the *Fort Severn* was anchored some hundred yards from shore. A motor-powered lifeboat provided the ferry service between the vessel and the post. The district manager enjoyed handling this little craft and whenever he was aboard, he took charge of starting the motor and handling the tiller. On my visits to the schooner I was so eager to get going that as soon as I stepped on board I pulled up the anchor. Since the anchor consisted of a rock and the chain consisted of a length of rope, once the rock was untied from the rope it became impossible to anchor the craft again.

Usually the motor started on the first pull of the cord so my impatience went unnoticed. But like all motors it had its balky periods. On the last night of the *Fort Severn*'s stay at Repulse it failed to start immediately. We began to drift. The district manager abandoned his motor-starting efforts long enough to give me a lecture on the why's and wherefore's of water safety. Then he yanked the cord again and the motor responded immediately.

The Journey Home

Finally, during the night the miracle I had been praying for happened. The ice dispersed sufficiently to allow passage from Repulse Bay. The lifeboat came ashore to pick up the passengers. I rushed to the mission to summon the Bishop. He was ready and appeared to be as eager as myself to avoid winter in the arctic. I scarcely had time to bid a hasty farewell to the Crawfords before I found myself in the lifeboat with my hand on the anchor rope, impatiently waiting for the throb of the motor. The clang of the chain from the raising anchor commenced while the Bishop and myself were still boarding the vessel. The *Fort Severn* began a dash for the open waters of Ross Welcome. We eased through the ice pack at the mouth of Repulse Bay. The ice lay waiting for a favorable wind and an incoming tide to take it home. Once that happened it would remain there, firmly entrenched throughout the winter.

The post manager who was scheduled to spend the next portion of his fur-trading career at Igloolik, arrived at Repulse with one main topic of conversation. If a person had a certificate showing him to be unfit for military service, he could take his pick of jobs, and what the money firms were willing to pay those unfit for military duty was nothing short of fantastic.

Now he had a second topic. He decided to duplicate Tom Crawford's happily married status. He anticipated no difficulty in being accepted by the girl of his choice while he waited at Churchill for a plane to take him to Igloolik.

Many members of the crew were former acquaintances from York Factory, Churchill and my trip into Repulse. One of these chaps had been promoted to first mate. Some of the familiar faces, however, had been replaced by Metis from Churchill and were serving as deckhands. I overheard one of these fellows beefing to his mate about the long layover at Repulse.

"What's your hurry?" replied his buddy. "You're getting paid by the day ain'tcha?"

"Yes, but I want to build a house," came the reply.

"So what?" The other saw no need for panic. "We'll be home a good week before freeze-up."

"Ya, but I wanna build a good house. I wanna take a couple of weeks to build it."

We made an overnight stop at Chesterfield Inlet. This time, however, I remained on the boat. Even so, I found that the head cold I had abandoned over a year ago was still faithfully waiting. It embraced me with all its miseries. Even a cold germ draws the line at the sixty-third parallel.

We arrived at the Churchill wharf around noon. There had obviously been some changes since I'd left. One of the chaps I knew as a member of the York Factory boat-building crew stood on the dock. A deck hand from the vessel threw him a tie rope. The rope landed on the wharf and lay there. A curse in Cree came from the ship. The ex-York Factory Metis took out his watch.

"Five to one," he said. "I don't start work for another five minutes."

There was no doubt about it. I had arrived back in civilization where everything functioned by clockwork. The deck hand who was about to turn housebuilder jumped onto the wharf and secured the ship.

Bob Urquhart wanted to take a vacation. Since I knew my way around Churchill, arrangements were made for the next train to leave town without me. Still, I had no overwhelming desire to get to Winnipeg. Churchill was a real whoop-her-up settlement, provided you could find the her. It wouldn't hurt in the least to enjoy myself for a month while I eased back into the ways of the outside world. I had no need to rush to acquire one of the excellent positions the new post manager at Igloolik had been telling me about. Since I was already rejected by both the Air Force and the Signal Corps I would have no difficulty in obtaining an "unfit for service" letter.

Just as I remembered it, life at Churchill proved to be anything but dull. Hudson's Bay Company business boomed and social life abounded. Since my previous posting to Manitoba's seaport, Bob had built up the business to the point that it now required both an apprentice and a female clerk to serve the customers.

At Churchill every event warranted a party. Bob Urquhart's holiday was an event. The party took place on the Sunday evening prior to the train's departure. After a couple of drinks the lonely post manager selected the girl of his dreams. He had no doubt that his choice would be overjoyed to accompany him to his post where she could convert the living quarters into a cozy home. The girl, however, had decidedly different ideas of her own. Since oral persuasion failed, he decided to drag her into his den by using caveman tactics. She broke free from his grasp. I suddenly found her sitting on my lap. Her unilaterally decreed husband-to-be came charging after her like a stampeding bull. I extended both my arms to ward off the rush. He attempted to leap over the barricade. My locked elbows caused his leap to extend upwards as if I had lifted him a couple of feet off the floor. However, what goes up must come down. And down he came. The realization of how stupid he looked from his sitting position in the center of the floor caused him to silently return to his room in the hotel. Two days later, when he left for Igloolik, he had not resumed speaking to me.

During Bob's absence I began to fill some of the evenings by playing bridge in the home of one of the local couples. I found that these games offered far more challenge than those at Repulse. They proved to be most enjoyable. However, during the chit chat that followed the serious bridge talk, I casually mentioned that I had two white fox pelts that I intended to have tanned. After the next bridge session the wife stretched herself out on the chesterfield and advised that her husband had no objections to her dating other men. It was the type of situation that separates men from boys. I decided I was still a boy. I bade a hasty goodnight and retreated. The next day I sold my pelts to the opposition trader. I had no desire to continue being the type of man who had what it took. For the balance of my tenure at Churchill, I had lost a customer for the Hudson's Bay post.

Since I was quartered at the hotel I received my meals when the proprietress decided a meal period was essential. Her breakfast period occurred at a time when, according to my list of priorities, sleep held a much higher position than food. Once I arrived at the store, any nourishment I required could be obtained by washing down salted peanuts with pop.

One morning my favorite assistant informed me that her mother wanted to have a word with me. As the girl and I had not been indulging in anything that could be construed as an affair I wondered what the problem could be. However, it turned out that her Scandinavian mother felt that I required more nourishment than peanuts and pop. She insisted I eat a full breakfast beginning with porridge and ending with bacon and eggs. As much as I enjoyed her breakfast over that served by my boarding place, from then on I rose early enough to eat breakfast in the establishment that was paid to feed me.

Before I managed to lose any more of the Hudson's Bay Company's customers Bob Urquhart returned from his vacation. The next day I was on the train to Winnipeg and four days later I arrived in Souris. I had money deposited in the bank and a million-dollar experience banked in my memory.

As the Igloolik manager had reported, the economy was booming.

Jobs were plentiful. But employers were reluctant to hire anyone who might enlist before he became fully trained. A military service rejection slip was a bigger asset than a university degree.

Since I considered myself to be well-qualified for this important document I took advantage of the mobile Air Force recruiting unit that visited my home town. I failed to obtain the sought-after piece of paper. The medical officer ran his cold hand over my naked body. "This one's warm," he said to his orderly. "Sign it up."

THE LONESOME LAKE
BELLA COOLA **TRILOGY**

Ralph Edwards of Lonesome Lake
by Ed Gould
The biography of the man who saved the
trumpeter swans.
5½x8½, 296 pp., 14 color and 56 b&w photos.
ISBN 0-88839-100-5
pb $9.95

Fogswamp
Living with Swans in the Wilderness
by Trudy Turner & Ruth M. McVeigh
Trudy, daughter of Ralph Edwards, continues
the saga.
5½x8½, 255 pp., 8 p. color, 32 p. b&w photos.
ISBN 0-88839-104-8
pb $9.95

Ruffles on my Longjohns
by Isabel Edwards
Candid autobiography of a woman pioneer.
5½x8½, 297 pp., 32 b&w photos.
ISBN 0-88839-102-1
pb $9.95

NATURE GUIDES BY HANCOCK HOUSE

WESTERN TITLES

Roadside Wildflowers of the Northwest
Ted Underhill

Northwestern Wild Berries
Ted Underhill

Western Mushrooms
Ted Underhill

Coastal Lowlands Wildflowers
Ted Underhill

Upland Forest Wildflowers
Ted Underhill

Sagebrush Wildflowers
Ted Underhill

Alpine Wildflowers
Ted Underhill

Wild Harvest
Terry Domico

Rocks and Minerals of the Northwest
Stan and Chris Learning

Birds of B.C.
D. Stirling and D. Hancock

Birds of the Prairie Provinces
D. Stirling and D. Hancock

Western Wildlife
David Hancock

Wildlife of the Rockies
David Hancock

Tidepool and Reef
Rick Harbo

Rocky Mountain Wildlife
Don Blood

EASTERN TITLES

Eastern Mushrooms
Barrie Kavasch

Eastern Roadside Wildflowers
Barrie Kavasch

Eastern Wildflowers
Barrie Kavasch

Northeastern Wild Edibles
Barrie Kavasch

Eastern Rocks and Minerals
Jim Grandy

Eastern Seashells
Townsend and Weekes

Eastern Wildlife
David Hancock

NATIONAL TITLES

Orchids of North America
Dr. Wm. Petrie

Indian Herbs
Dr. Raymond Stark

EASTERN FISHING SERIES

Secrets of Baitfishing
D. W. Bennett

Secrets of Bluefishing
D. W. Bennett

Secrets of Striped Bass Fishing
D. W. Bennett

Secrets of Bottom Fishing
Ed Ricciuti

Secrets of Potfishing
Ed Ricciuti

Secrets of Shellfishing
Ed Ricciuti

Fish of the Atlantic
B. Freeman

**SEND SELF-ADDRESSED ENVELOPE TO PUBLISHER
FOR FULL CATALOG.**

INDIAN TITLES BY HANCOCK HOUSE

NATIVE HUNTER SERIES
Dr. Stephen Irwin

Hunters of the Ice
Hunters of the Northern Forest
Hunters of the Buffalo
Hunters of the Sea
Hunters of the Eastern Forest

ART AND CULTURE SERIES

Haida
Leslie Drew

Coast Salish
Reg Ashwell

Tlingit
Nan Kaiper Slygh

Iroquois
Carrie Lyford

Blackfeet
John Ewers

GENERAL TITLES

American Indian Pottery
Sharon Wirt

Argillite
Leslie Drew and Douglas Wilson

Indian Artifacts of the Northeast
Roger Moeller

Artifacts of the Northwest Indians
Hilary Stewart

Art of the Totem
Marius Barbeau

Eskimo Life of Yesterday
Revillon Freres

Images: Stone: B.C.
Wilson Duff

Indian Art and Culture
Kew and Goddard

Indian Healing
Dr. Wolfgang Jilek

Indians of the Northwest Coast
D. Allen

Indian Petroglyphs of the Pacific Northwest
Beth Hill

Indian Rock Carvings of the Pacific Northwest Coast
Beth Hill

Indian Tribes of the Northwest
Reg Ashwell

Indian Weaving, Knitting and Basketry of the Northwest
Elizabeth Hawkins

Kwakiutl Legends
Chief James Wallas

Life With the Eskimos
A photo essay

My Heart Soars
Chief Dan George

My Spirit Soars
Chief Dan George

North American Indians
A photographic study

The Providers
Dr. Stephen Irwin

Song of Creation
Helmut Hirnschall

Those Born at Koona
John and Carolyn Smyly

Totem Poles of the Northwest
D. Allen

We-gyet Wanders On
Gitksan People

Western Indian Basketry
Joan Megan Jones

**SEND SELF-ADDRESSED ENVELOPE TO PUBLISHER
FOR FULL CATALOG.**